D1624279

Neal Donald Walsch:

On Relationships: Of course we can not relate to others in any meaningful way unless and until we relate to ourselves and to our own daily experience in a way which reflects the truth of who we are.

On Holistic Living: The first step in holistic living is forgiveness. And until we have learned the Divine Healing, until we've used the balm of forgiveness on our wounds, those wounds will fester inside of us long after the outward scars have apparently disappeared.

On Abundance: True abundance has nothing to do with anything that I am having, and everything to do with what I am being.

On Right Livelihood: Be who you are in every moment of your life. Come from that place, and let your doingness spring from that place. And you'll not only find right livelihood, you will have created for yourself a life, rather than a living.

NEALE DONALD WALSCH'S

LITTLE BOOK OF
LIFE

NEALE DONALD WALSCH'S
LITTLE BOOK OF
LIFE

A USER'S MANUAL

by the author of the
New York Times bestselling
Conversations with God

NEALE DONALD WALSCH

BRISTOL
PARK
BOOKS

The material in this book was previously published by Hampton
Roads as *Neale Donald Walsch on Relationships, Neale Donald
Walsch on Abundance and Right Livelihood* and *Neale Donald
Walsch on Holistic Living*

First Bristol Park Books edition published in 2013

Bristol Park Books
252 W. 38th Street
NYC, NY 10018

Bristol Park Books is a registered trademark of Bristol Park
Books, Inc.

Published by arrangement with Hampton Roads Publishing Company

Cover and text design by Frame25 Productions
Cover Art by PKruger c/o Shutterstock.com

ISBN: 978-0-88486-522-3

Printed in the United States of America.

Contents

Introduction

This life is such a mystery. At least it *feels* that way. There's so much to figure out, so much to know about, so much to understand. And then, when you finally do understand it, there seems to be so *little* to figure out, and there's no mystery at all . . . .

I'm describing to you my own experience before and after my conversations with God. Those dialogues told me everything I needed to know about life, and helped me to understand so much of what I didn't understand. And when I put those exchanges into a book and people all over the world began reading them, life changed for many of us. The messages in what became the nine *Conversations with God* books had an enormous impact on millions of people in many cultures because they made everything so clear.

Perhaps predictably, I was soon asked to elaborate on that original material, to address more extensively what I had experienced, as well as what I had come to discover *through* my experience. I decided to take the information in the three thousand pages of my original dialogue and explore it more fully, topic by topic. The book you are now holding is a result of that decision.

This text is a re-issue of material that I published more than a decade ago, in three separate volumes. I believe that information to be seminal, pivotal, and vital to any real understanding of how to *apply* the wisdom in *Conversations with God* to our everyday lives. I have brought the material together under one cover here because, while the three original small volumes were helpful, to be sure, I see on reflection that *taken together* they lay out an entire course for living well; first, for living harmoniously and lovingly with others in our immediate circle, then with ourselves and our work, and finally, with the World Entire.

If ever there was a time for such a course to be laid, this would be it. The world is hovering on the brink of its next major evolutionary convulsion—a giving birth, as futurist Barbara Marx Hubbard would put it—a full-scale creation of a new way of being human. And while I don't consider myself to be an expert on sociological or spiritual development within our species, I do believe the guidelines offered here to be among the most useful, the most practical, and the most effective tools that anyone could ever find for producing a better life. I feel that way because I am not the source of these guidelines. The messages here emerge solely from the *Conversations with God* dialogues—and I consider those exchanges to have been direct interactions with the Divine.

You do not have to agree with me on that point, however. As I have said often in the past, it is not necessary to believe that I spoke directly with God (we are all doing this every day, by the way) in order to gain benefit from this material. All that is required is an open mind and a willingness to simply see if the ideas here have any value. Use them, *test them out*, in on-the-ground situations.

That's what I invite you to do. I encourage you to take a look at what's being said here about the three aspects of our lives—relationships, livelihood, and our interactions with the world at large—and see for yourself if anything here makes sense; if *any* of it is workable, practical, and beneficial.

Of course, I believe that it all is or I wouldn't be placing it before you, much less inviting you to spend any serious amount of time exploring it. So here you have it: the three thousand pages of dialogue in *Conversations with God* reduced down to a few salient points and a few very direct observations about how to render them functional. I trust that you will find this deeper excursion into *Conversations with God* spiritually enticing, personally exciting, and wonderfully useful.

Part One

Living and Interacting with Others

Introduction

Relationships are the most important experience of our lives. Without it, we are nothing.

Literally.

That is because, in the absence of anything else, we are not.

Fortunately, there is not a one of us who does not have a relationship. Indeed, all of us are in relationships with everything and everyone, all of the time. We have a relationship with ourselves, we have a relationship with our family, we have a relationship with our environment, we have a relationship with our work, we have a relationship with each other.

In fact, everything that we know and experience about ourselves, we understand within the context that is created by our relationships. For this reason, relationships are sacred. All relationships. And somewhere within the deepest reaches of our heart and soul, we know this. That is why we yearn so for relationships—and for relationships of meaning. It is also, no doubt, why we have such trouble with them. At some level, we must be very clear how much is at stake. And so, we're nervous about them. Normally confident, competent people fumble and fall, stumble and stall, crumble and call for help.

Indeed, nothing has caused more problems for our species, created more pain, produced more suffering, or resulted in more tragedy, than that which was intended to bring us our greatest joy—our relationships with each other. Neither individually nor collectively, socially nor politically, locally nor internationally have we found a way to live in harmony. We simply find it very difficult to get along—much less actually love each other.

What's this all about? What's up here? I think I know. Not that I'm some kind of a genius, mind you, but I am a good listener. And I've been asking questions about this for a very long time. In the 1980s, I began receiving answers. I believe those responses have come from God. At the time I received them, I was so impacted and so impressed that I decided to keep a written record of what I was being given. That record became the *Conversations with God* series of books, which have become bestsellers around the world.

A small group of about forty people gathered at a home just outside San Francisco, California a few years ago to explore with me more deeply what those books had to say on the subject of our relationships with others. I shared with the group all that I understood about the material on relationships that appears in the *Conversations with God* dialogue and answered questions as they came up. The synergy of that afternoon produced an electrifying experience, resulting in an open flow of wonderful wisdom that, I am happy to say, was captured on videotape and audiocassette—edited versions of which have since been made available to the public.

What you will find here is a transcript of that event. I have made a few tiny edits in order to update it to my present life circumstance, but no substantive changes have been made. Thus, the material reads in a much more free-flowing—and, I think, more stimulating—style than text that is written for the printed page. And because this book format is not limited by time and production constraints, we were able to include here material not found in the original video or audio versions, which necessarily had to be shortened for production reasons.

Essentially, what God tells us in *Conversations with God* is that most of us enter into relationships for the wrong reasons. That is, for reasons having nothing to do with our overall *life purpose*. When our reason for relationships is aligned with our soul's reason for being, not only are our relationships understood to be sacred, they are rendered joyful as well.

Joyful relationships—ah, yes. For far too many people, that phrase sounds almost like an oxymoron—a self-contradicting, mutually exclusive term. Something like *military intelligence* or *efficient government*. Yet it *is* possible to have joyful relationships, and the extraordinary insights in the *Conversations with God* books show us how.

Here are those insights, as I have received them and understood them. I share them with you here in humility, straight from the Take It For What It's Worth Department, with the hope that if even one comment opens a new window—or throws wide a doorway—to greater happiness, you will have been served.

Hello, everyone. Welcome to the room. Nice to see you all here.

The subject of the moment is human relationships, this thing with which some of us have so much difficulty. No one, I understand, in this room, but some of the rest of us have had some difficulty with this topic. And as you know, if you've read any of the writings that have come from my pen, I'm among those who have had some considerable difficulty in relationships—in making them work, and making them last, and really, in causing them to even make any sense in my life.

I've never really understood, until these most recent days and times, what makes relationships work, and what their purpose is in my life. And the reason that was true for me is that, in the main, I found myself getting into relationships for all the wrong reasons.

By and large, I got *into* relationships with an eye toward what I could get *out* of them. And I'm not even sure I was willing to admit that to myself as I was getting into these relationships. I mean, I probably wouldn't have articulated it that way, because I didn't want myself to know myself. I wouldn't have said, "Gee, what is it I'm trying to get out of this?" I wouldn't have phrased it that way. I probably wouldn't even have conceptualized it in that way. But I noticed that's what I was up to, as soon as I stopped getting out of the relationship what I imagined that I would. In the moment that I stopped getting out of the relationship what I imagined that I would, *I* wanted to get out of the relationship.

And that's the pattern that I saw myself running through the largest portion of my adult life. I got out of relationships from which I did not get what I wanted. Did you follow that? And I got *into* relationships after I got out of other ones. Very quickly. So, I was a serial monogamist. Just one relationship after another, after another, after another, seeking and searching for that right and perfect mate who could, at last, fulfill me. Who could maybe see who I really am, and bring me to a place of happiness.

Now, I was willing to make a fair trade. It wasn't that I wasn't willing to show up in certain ways that could cause me to be attractive to another. Quite the contrary, I knew how the game was played. And after a few failed relationships, I even began to know, or to think that I knew, what it was that others were looking for in a relationship. And so I worked very hard to provide that for them—as my negotiable goods, see. I learned, for instance, to sublimate certain parts of my own personality that I discovered, after a number of failed relationships, were not attractive to other people.

I'll give you one example, a silly one, but it's one that sticks with me because of its silliness, I think. I was with one lady for a while, and I thought she was going to be the love of my life. In fact, she *was* the love of my life during that time of my life I was with her.

So, I was in this particular relationship with this delicious lady. And I was deeply in love. And we went to the theater one night, in one of our early excursions into the outer world, the world of social stuff, you know. And so there I was at this play. And it was a comedy, and I began to laugh.

Now, I happen to have a very raucous, uproarious laugh. When I laugh, the whole room knows that I have laughed, unlike most of you, who aren't laughing very loudly at all, at any of this.

When I laugh, I really have this whole-feeling laughter. And it's just been part of me. I didn't design it that way; this is just how it is. Okay. So, here I am, and I'm roaring. Now, the players are, of course, loving it, because it's generating other laughter, and the room is becoming very alive. And so the actors are thrilled that in the audience they have what they call, as an actor, a live wire. "We've got a live wire in the house tonight."

So, I'm always welcome in places where there are performers, because I'm a real live wire. But the lady that I was with, and with whom I was so desperately in love (and I use that term advisedly—I was desperate *about* my love for her)—the more I laughed, the smaller she got. I can still see her to this day, sitting in the seat next to me, trying to disappear. And during intermission, she said, "Must you laugh like that?" And I remember thinking, "Like what?" because I wasn't even consciously aware, you know, of what I was doing; that my laughter was causing her embarrassment. That it was, as we used to say as teenagers, spotting her out. That she felt somehow on the spot because of this guy she was with who was laughing in that way.

And I remember my deep desire to do whatever it took to keep her in the room. You know what I mean? I mean, figuratively, to keep her in the room of my life.

By the way, I should say, as an aside, I spent most of my life trying to keep people in the room. I would do almost anything. Just stay in the room. Stay in the room. Don't leave the room. What can I do to keep you here? What part of myself can I set aside to keep you here? It's of no matter. I'll set it aside. All that matters is, stay in the room of my life.

And I can't tell you the number of tap dances that I did—and not even to my own music. You put the music on, and I'll dance the dance. And I did that on this particular night at the theater.

Now comes act two, and I'm in the audience. And here come a few funny gag lines, and this is the action you're getting from Neale . . . ha . . . [sputtering] . . . sitting there trying to stifle my laugh. By act three, I had it down. By act three, I had turned "ha, ha, ha, ha" into a quiet "hee, hee . . ." And for several years, that's how I laughed. I used to laugh what I called a non-laugh, until somebody said: "Is something wrong with you? Are you okay?"

I was in a workshop with Dr. Elisabeth Kübler-Ross once, and she caught me at that. She called my number. She said something funny, and I was out there in the first row. She said, "What's the matter with you?"

"Nothing; I thought that was funny."

She said, "Why didn't you let that out?"

Anyone know Elisabeth Kübler-Ross? Very heavy Swiss accent. I became close friends with her. I wound up working on her staff. Let that be a warning; some of you may be on my staff before the day is out.

And she said, "Why don't you let that out?" Or, in her Swiss accent, "Vy don't you let dat laughter out?"

And I said: "What do you mean? I was laughing."

She says: "No, you weren't. Why don't you let that laughter out? And while you're at it, why don't you let the pain out as well? The pain of holding in Who You Really Are?"

So I was aware of what needed to be traded, or what I thought needed to be traded, to keep you in the room, you see. I was not unaware, and I was not unwilling. So, I did what I thought it took to keep the room filled. And that was the great puzzlement for me, because here I was doing what I thought it took to keep the room filled, and the room kept on emptying anyway. They kept on leaving anyway, until I finally found myself screaming: "What do you want? What does it take to make a relationship work?"

And I didn't even catch the act. I didn't even see that I was, in fact, trading this for that. I'll tell you what: I won't laugh like this if you don't cough like that. See, I won't eat like this, if you don't forget to put the toothpaste cap on the tube . . . like that, or whatever it is that we were trading. And the trades were much larger than that, I'm afraid.

And so, I wound up in this kind of a trade arrangement, you know. And on the 14th of February, I searched and searched for a card; but I couldn't find one that said, "I trade you very much." "Gosh, do I trade you. And I'll trade you forever." But I was, in fact, playing trade. And again I knew that I was playing trade when the other person stopped trading me what I thought they were supposed to give me. That was our quid pro quo arrangement: I'll give you this, and you'll give me that. And when I stopped receiving what I thought I was supposed to receive, I left the relationship. Or, in some cases, when they stopped receiving what they thought was implicitly theirs, what they thought I was going to give them, they left the room.

And that's how I discovered that I was into relationships for all the wrong reasons, that I was somehow searching for that treasure, that negotiable currency that I could have which would be large enough to keep everyone in the room. What aspect of myself could be so attractive, so undeniable, so magnetic, that no matter what, you would stay in the room? And I didn't understand, until I had lost yet another in a series of important relationships, what was going wrong.

Then I had my extraordinary conversation with God, in which God said: "Neale, Neale, Neale, you clearly don't see what's going on here. First of all, you're in a relationship for all the wrong reasons. You're in a relationship for what you can get out of it. And you're willing to trade all right. But you see it as just that—almost a business transaction. And you don't understand the purpose of a relationship. And the purpose of a relationship has nothing to do with what you think you can get out of it, and everything to do with what you choose to put into it. But not putting something into it as a *means of extracting from it what you wish to receive,* but simply putting something into it as a means of noticing Who You Really Are.

So, what you put into a relationship, be sure that you put into it authentically. And never deny, for one moment, the real you. And if the real you isn't sufficient or attractive enough to keep that person in the room, then let them leave. Because someone will come into the room of your life who will find the authentic you attractive enough. And when they come into the room out of their response to your authenticity, they will stay because you don't have to keep your act going in order to keep them in the room, you see. And so the tap dance can be over.

And that changed everything for me in relationships. It shifted the whole paradigm of my experience, because at last I understood what I was doing there.

I also understood that relationships are the most important single experience we could possibly create for ourselves. And that in the absence of relationships, we are nothing. Without you, I am nothing at all. You probably knew that when you walked in. You sat down; "Without me, Neale's nothing" [laughter]. But it's true. Because without you, I'm nothing at all [pointing to different people]. And without you, I'm nothing. And without you, I'm nothing at all. And that is true, because absent the experience of relationship, we are not. In this relative experience, I can only be who I am in relationship to something else in my experience. I mean, experientially, I can't know a thing about myself unless you're in the room.

And I was given an interesting illustration by God that allowed me to notice how this could be true. God said to me: "Imagine that you were in an all-white room, totally white: white floor, white ceiling, white walls. And imagine you were suspended in that room, as if by magic, so that you couldn't touch anything, just dangling there, like so many Christmas ornaments, without even a string attaching you to it, just suspended in mid-air. Here you are in this sea of whiteness. And imagine that nothing else exists at all. How long do you think that you would exist in your own experience?" And the answer came up for me: "Probably not terribly long, not very long."

Because, in the absence of anything else, I am not. Not in my own experience. I mean, I am that I am. But I can't *know* that I am. I can't experience that I am, except in relationship to something else. So, I can't know anything about myself.

Yet, if somebody were to walk into that room of whiteness, and just put so much as the tiniest speck of ink on the wall, to the degree that I could see that speck of ink, that little black dot, to that degree suddenly I exist. First of all, *over there* would exist, and *over here*. Because the dot would be there, and I would be here. I would begin to define myself in relationship to that other thing. In this case, the dot on the wall. I would imagine that I am the thing called . . . Maybe I would utter a word that sounded like "big-g-ger."

I might even have the audacity to say, with regard to the dot on the wall, that I'm "sma-a-arter." Sometimes I don't think that I'm very much smarter than the dot on the wall, but generally speaking, I imagine that I am. I may be faster, or slower, or "this-er" or "that-er," you understand, in relationship to the dot.

Put a cat in the room, and suddenly I have much larger experiences of myself, because that which is also in the space is much larger than the dot on the wall. So now I begin to conceptualize all kinds of things about me. Maybe the cat is softer than I am, but maybe I am older than the cat, or whatever. You see, I start conceiving of myself in my own experience, based on who and what is around me. Therefore, relationships—I'm talking now in the realm of the relative, in which we exist in physical form—relationships with other people, places, and things are not only important, they are vital. And in the absence of our relationships with everything, we are not.

And so I begin to understand the reason that relationships exists at all: my relationships with this table, with this glass of water, and with those of you who share this time and place with me. And it is out of my relationship with you that I not only know myself—but here comes the trick—not only do I know myself out of my relationship with you, but I literally *define* myself as well. That is to say: I define and, in that sense, *re-create who I am* in relationship to Who You Are.

Here comes an interesting twist. Ultimately, I cannot re-create myself as anything that you are not. That is to say: I can only see in me what I'm willing to see in you. And that which I fail to see in you, I will never find in myself, because I don't know that it exists. Therefore, I cannot find the divinity within me until I seek, discover, and recognize (that is to say: know again, to re-*cognize*) the divinity in you. And to the degree that I fail to recognize and to know the divinity in you, to that degree I cannot know it in me, nor can I know any good thing about myself. Nor any bad thing either, for that matter. For nothing can exist over here that does not exist over there. And the reasons for that are multitudinous; not the least of which is, there is only one of us in the room. There's no one else here. So, we find that relationships have a unique place in our life, not just an important place—if I can use a twist of words—an irreplaceable place. I mean, you can't replace it. There's nothing that you can replace relationships with that will bring you what relationships bring you, because relationships are the only experience in life that brings you an experience of yourself in life. And we are talking here about not only your relationships to people, but also to places, and things, and even events—even your relationships to the occurrences of your life.

We all have relationships to the circumstances and the events of our lives. And it is out of our relationships, which are entirely self-created, that we experience, announce, and declare, express, fulfill, and become who we really are.

Once we understand the sacred place that relationship holds in the experience of all of us, we hold the experience of relationship as sacred in deed—not just in thought, not just in word, but in *deed*. And the deeds we do around relationships begin to change dramatically.

First we see the secret that I announced a moment ago: that only what I see in you can I see in me. And so it becomes our primary function in relationships, once this secret is understood, to look deeply at you, to see in you the grandest vision I could ever imagine; indeed, even to assist you in creating that, to the degree that you choose to avoid creating it. So one thing that partners do with and for each other is not seek to take from another, but seek to give to another, and to empower that other with whom you are partnered to express and experience who they really are, because we see the vital importance of that. And we see that that is, in fact, the *raison d'être* of all relationships, their very reason for being.

Suddenly our purpose in a relationship becomes entirely transmuted and transformed. We are no longer trying to find out what we can get from the relationship, but what we can give. What can we empower? What can we create? What can we cause to be realized, made real—be *real*-ized? You know how you Simoniz your car? You can *realize* people. You just shine them up a bit. And they become *real*-ized. And this, in the end, is the ultimate self-realization.

And that's the secret I want to share with you today. Many people are involved in the self-realization movement. And they think that self-realization is somehow achieved by sitting quietly by yourself. Because, after all, it's called *self*-realization. So, we're going to realize ourselves by sitting quietly by ourselves alone in a room, with a candle perhaps, and maybe some quiet music. And maybe we make some interesting sounds, you know, "Ohhhmmm." Whatever we do, and I'm not putting that down, I'm not making that wrong, but if you think that that is the way to self-realize and that the more hours you spend doing that . . . you will not have understood the grand wisdom: that we are for each other.

Ultimately, self-realization is not achieved alone. Self-realization is achieved when we realize the Self as seen in another. That is why all true masters do nothing but walk around, giving other people back to themselves. Have you ever been seen by a living master? Have you ever been in the presence of someone that you considered a spiritual master, or as close to it as we're going to get in this lifetime? Have you been in the room with someone who is working toward that level of self-mastery? If you have (and you'll recognize them at once), you will notice that they spend the majority of their days and times seeing mastery in you. They will look at you, look in your eyes, and see you as even you do not imagine yourself to be. And you'll wonder why *you* don't see you as they see you. Then *they* will wonder why you don't see you. I'll try that again. [laugh] This is obviously a statement I'm not supposed to make. Are we all ready to be quiet? Then they will wonder why they do not . . . And they will wonder why you do not . . . forget it . . . [laughs]. I know when the elements have defeated me.

When we use a relationship in this delicious way, we transform our whole experience of ourselves with our loved ones. Suddenly, we want nothing *from* them—and only want to give everything *to* them. And we seek to give everything we are to them, needing nothing in return.

Now, be clear. This doesn't mean we allow them to walk all over us. This doesn't mean we allow ourselves to be somehow the victims in a relationship that's dysfunctional with them. That's not what we're talking about here. Life does not require us to stay in the same room with someone who is abusing us. And that's why I'm leaving this room right now. You could laugh a little more loudly at my jokes . . . .

But it does mean that as we give of ourselves to others in the fullest measure, we allow ourselves the experience of a love which knows no condition, even as we say, "I choose not to co-reside with you." See, one of these days we'll even find a way to do the thing called separate from each other without bitterness. See, we won't need attorneys. You know the only reason we need lawyers? Because there are lawyers.

One of these days we'll be able to look at each other and say: "I notice now that our time together is concluded. I notice now that it's the moment for us to continue to love each other without condition, to continue to give each other the gifts that are ours to give in fullness, and yet, to do so from across the room, or across the street, or from around the world. Because certain of your physical behaviors are not in harmony with how I choose to live my life. And that doesn't mean that I don't love you."

One of these days, we'll be able to speak that truth without having to somehow find something wrong with the other, or make them the villain of the piece in order to justify our truth. When we can get to that place, we can also create, then, the loving, enduring relationships that we long for in our lives, because those relationships, too, are suddenly hinged on no condition whatsoever, and no limitation, either.

Here's what I know about the best relationships, and how they work. First of all, they are relationships that know no condition. There is no conditionality to the best relationships. There is no limitation. Because relationships that are based in real love—a love which is true—are relationships which are totally and completely free.

Freedom is the essence of Who You Are. Freedom is the essence of love. The word *love* and the word *freedom* are interchangeable. As is the word *joy*. Joy, love, freedom—love, freedom, love, joy. They all mean the same thing. And the human soul cannot be joyful to the degree that it's restricted or limited in any way.

Therefore, when we love another, we never ever seek to limit or restrict them in any way whatsoever. Love says, "My will for you is your will for you." Love says, "I choose for you what you choose for you." When I say, "I choose for you what *I* choose for you," then I'm not loving you. I'm loving me through you, because I'm getting what I want, rather than seeing you get what you want.

Here is the supreme irony of that paradigm: the moment that I say, "I choose for you what you choose for you," you will never leave me. Because all we are searching for is someone who will let us have what we want out of life. See, the whole world contrives to not let us have what we want out of life, starting with our parents, at the age of two. "No, can't have that." It went on to our teachers in school. "Do not chew gum in class." And much larger restrictions, thank you very much.

It continued through our adolescent years, when our budding sexuality caused us to want one thing and the world contrived to demonstrate to us that it was somehow inappropriate to want that—in some religions, to even desire it. Oh, what havoc we have wreaked on this planet with our insane sexual stuff. Insanity.

And it continued in our young-adult years, and even into the later days of our adulthood, with the world contriving to tell us we cannot have what we really want. I mean, I even know some wives who actually go to some husbands, and say: "Honey, there's a quilting class down at the Y. It's every Tuesday night for six weeks. I'd like to take it." And I actually know some husbands who say no. Can you imagine a husband saying to a wife, "I don't want you taking that quilting class"? Yet, it happens.

"Archie. It's just a quilting class, Arch."

"Stifle it. Stifle yourself, Edith."

Remember that? And the reason that the whole country laughed at Archie Bunker was that half the country saw itself there. And it was an embarrassed laugh.

I had a father—God rest his soul—and I love him dearly, but he was very, very much like that. He wasn't quite Archie Bunker-ish in some ways; he didn't have those racial ideas or thoughts, but, boy, did he have the thoughts: "I'm the ruler of the house. And she can't take a quilting class without my permission, and I will rarely give it."

In a relationship that is constructed around a genuine expression of real love, not only is it okay if the wife comes to the husband and says, "Can I take a quilting class?" it's also okay if the wife comes to the husband and says: "Can I have lunch with Harry? And by the way, my darling, your name is not Harry." And the husband, we'll call him Mike, says: "My will for you is your will for you. You want to have lunch with Harry, have lunch with Harry. I love you enough to want for you what you want for you."

If Harry has any thought of somehow stealing that person from Mike, he might as well forget it, because the number of people who are going to leave the Mikes, who give them that kind of freedom to express themselves, is minuscule. But huge is the number of women who will walk away from Mike immediately if Mike says: "You can't have lunch with Harry—in fact, don't even mention his name in this house! Don't even think about it—what's the matter with you anyway? Don't you realize that you belong to me? You're my woman."

Women do this to men, too, incidentally. "By the way, sweetheart, I'd like to have lunch with Matilda." "I don't think so." I use a silly, way-out example to make a point. Life will bring you these opportunities in large quantities to demonstrate Who You Really Are.

Love never says no. You know how I know that? Because God never says no. And God and love are interchangeable.

God would never say no to you, no matter what your request. Even if God thought that what you're asking for is going to get you into trouble. Like Matilda. Or Harry. Or anything else. See, God will never say no, because God realizes that ultimately you can't get into the biggest trouble. That is to say, you can't damage yourself in a way that causes you not to be. You can only evolve and grow, become more of Who You Really Are. So, God says to us: "I choose for you what you choose for you. And I dare you to do that with those whom *you* love."

Now, wake up. I want you all to wake up. Because I want you to know, you'll start falling asleep as soon as you are confronted with that which you do not want to hear. You literally start falling asleep right in your chair [laugh]. And you'll think, of course, that it's to do with something else other than what he's talking about. "I'm just tired." That is the mechanism of the subconscious when it starts confronting data that it does not want to fully receive or embrace. "I'll just sleep through this part." Be careful, because most of us are sleepwalking through life. So, be careful you don't spend your life sleepwalking. Stay awake. Stay awake. You do not know the hour that your master will come.

There's a question in the audience on this delicate subject of relationship. Let us see what that question is . . . .

Neale, in Book 3 *of* Conversations with God, *you asked God about the institution of marriage. And . . . God nixed it, said that it didn't have a lot of validity. Do you believe that?*

Well, I think you misread what God had to say there. God did not say that marriage has no validity, and God did not nix it. God said that marriage, the way you are currently constructing it . . .

The institution.

Well, even the institution, *the way you've currently devised it*—not the institution per se, and not marriage per se, but marriage the way you [society] have constructed it, the way you have devised it—has no validity, given where you say you want to go.

Validity itself is a relative term. Relative to what? Valid relative to what? See, God says there's no such thing as right or wrong, believe it or not, because *right* and *wrong* are relative terms. A thing that is right yesterday is wrong today, and vice versa. And life has demonstrated that to us amply.

We don't need to go into that here. Any thinking person understands that right and wrong are relative terms. And God uses the terms *right* and *wrong,* or *valid* or *invalid,* relative to what we are announcing and declaring that we are choosing for ourselves, as a species and as individuals.

We have announced and declared that we choose for ourselves for marriage to be the highest expression of the grandest experience of love of which humans are capable. That's what we've said. We have said, "We choose for marriage to be an expression of the grandest and highest love of which humans are capable." Then we proceed to construct a marriage institution and a marriage experience which produces exactly the opposite of that—virtually the lowest form of love of which humans are capable. A love that possesses rather than releases. A love that limits rather than expands. A love that owns rather than disowns. A love that makes virtually everything around it smaller rather than making everything around it larger.

We've created an experience of marriage that has nothing to do with love in far too many instances. We've created a holder, a shell, some kind of an encasement. And that's what we want marriage to be. We want it to be an encasement that holds everything exactly where it was the moment we said, "I love you," and that holds us all exactly where we were in that first moment. But people and events move around. They change. Life is an evolution. And so marriage, as we have constructed it, works against the very process of life itself, because it provides very little breathing room in the way many societies and religions and family traditions have constructed it.

Largely, marriage has been used by those societies, religions, and families as a mini-prison, as kind of a contractual arrangement that says: "Everything will be, now and forevermore, the way it is in just this moment. You will love no one else, and you certainly won't demonstrate that love for anyone else in the way you demonstrate your love for me. You won't go anywhere else except where I go. You'll do very little that I do not do with you, and in most ways from this day forward, your life is going to be, at least to some degree, limited." And so the very thing which should unlimit people and release the spirit within them, works against that and limits people and closes that spirit down.

That's the irony of marriage as we've created it. We say, "I do," and from the moment we say, "I do," we *can't* do the things that we would really love to do in life, in largest measure. Now, very few people would admit this in the first throes of romance and in the first moments after their wedding. They would only come to these conclusions three, or five, or—what's the famous phrase, *the seven-year itch*—seven years later, when they suddenly realize that, in fact, their experience of themselves in the world at large has been reduced, and *not* enlarged, by the institution of marriage.

That's not true, of course, in all marriages, naturally. But it's true in enough of them—I'm going to say, in the majority of them. And that is why we have such a high divorce rate, because it isn't so much that people have gotten tired of each *other,* not nearly so often as they've gotten tired of the *restrictions* and the *limitations* that marriage seems to have imposed upon them. The human heart knows when it's being asked to be less.

Now love, on the other hand, is all about freedom. The very definition of love is freedom itself. Love is that which is free and knows no limitation, restriction, or condition of any kind. And so I think that what we have done here is that we have created an artificial construction around that which is least artificial. Love is the most authentic experience within the framework of the human adventure. And yet in the midst of this grand authenticity, we have created these artificial constrictions. And that makes it very difficult for people to stay in love.

And so what we have to do is reconstruct marriage, if we're going to have marriage at all, in a way that says: "I do not limit you. There is no condition that makes it okay for us to remain together. I do not have any desire to cause you to be less in your expression of yourself, in any way. Indeed, what this marriage is intended to do, this new form of marriage, is to fuel the engine of your experience—the experience of who you really are and who you choose to be."

And one last thing that the New Marriage does: it says, "I recognize that even you, yourself, will change. Your ideas will change, your tastes will change, your desires will change. Your whole understanding of Who You Are had *better* change, because if it doesn't change, you've become a very static personality over a great many years, and nothing would displease me more. And so I recognize that the process of evolution will produce changes in you."

This new form of marriage not only allows for such changes, but it encourages them.

Your old construction of the institution of marriage, given what you say you want to do and what you want it to be, is invalid. That is not a valid way to produce that. And yet, we're still trying to produce that in our daily lives, with the old way we have constructed marriages.

Even the marriage vows, some of the traditional marriage vows (thank goodness we've changed a few of them through the years), but even some of the marriage vows, for centuries, talked in terms of ownership and created philosophical constructions that couldn't possibly support what true love would choose to create.

And young people, by the way, know this. Young people know this instinctively, which is why for years, and increasingly in the sixties, seventies, and eighties, young people would look at older people and say: "You know, we're not buying it. We're not doing it. We're not going there."

And so they did this thing called live together, which of course, in the sixties and seventies was looked at like "How can they do that?" In the late fifties, in 1958, if you lived with someone, it was a scandal. But soon, kids were doing it right and left, saying: "You know, you can take your idea of marriage and toss it, because we don't get it. We get that love does not limit, does not own, does not hold in, but expands, lets go, and releases the grandest part of who all of us are."

And so, as has been the case really from the beginning of time, whenever any major change has been made in society, it has been the babes among us, the children among us, who showed us. It was not us old fuddy-duddies with all this gray in our hair, but it was, by and large, the young among us who said: "We know, and we can show you, a better way. And now we're going to do that."

As we see this huge shift into the twenty-first century, we notice that not only are—this is really the funny part—not only are the young people, the teenagers and the just-after-teenagers, living together, but so, too, are older folks. The eighty-, and seventy-, and sixty-five-year-olds are looking at each other, going: "Well, Martha, they're doing it. Why don't we do it? Let's just live together." And a shocking number of sixty-five-, and seventy-, and eighty-year-old women are actually saying, "Well, why not?"

Now, this is not an argument against marriage as an institution. Let's be clear. This is an exploration of what we've created the institution of marriage to be in the largest number of cases. There are many marriages that are created in such a loving way that there's no sense of conditionality or limitation to them. My wife and I will not allow our love to be conditioned by any particular response or set of responses, or any particular behavior, but rather there is only one behavior that my partner and I require of each other: "*Live authentically.* Live your truth. And if you love me for anything, love me because I live mine." Can you hear that? That's when you know you're in a blessed relationship.

I once turned to a wonderful lady to whom I was married and said something that I was struck with. I looked at her quite spontaneously one day and said, "You know, living with you is like living alone." That's a grand thing to say. Because I am most authentic, you know, most myself, when there's no one else around. I might get out of bed and walk around naked for a whole ten minutes. I may even sneak down to the kitchen with no clothes on, or jump into the pool. I may say certain things; I may sing a song; I may . . . I may just do stuff, just *be* in ways that I have this imagined idea that I can only be and do when I'm totally alone. If you're living with a really delicious person you'll experience that being with them is like being alone.

Such a person can literally give you back to yourself. You know you are with such a person when they say, "You know how I love you most?"

You say, "No. How?"

And they say, "Just the way you're showing up now."

"You mean, overweight and all? Big laugh and all?"

"I not only love you in spite of your laughter, I love you because of it. I not only love you in spite of what you imagine your faults to be, I love you because of them."

That's love. Everything else is counterfeit.

By the way, do you know what faults are? (I left my handkerchief somewhere else, and I can't even cry now at my own material.) Do you know what faults are? [Someone hands him a tissue.] Thank you very much. False evidence appearing real, for sure. But that's FEAR—False Evidence Appearing Real. I used to think that I was a person with all these faults, and that's why I couldn't make relationships work.

I used to think, "If only I straightened myself out, then I could present myself in a package that you would endure, if not enjoy." Because I thought that I had all these faults, because all these people in my life, including (God bless them) my parents some of the time, were telling me about all the faults that I had, you know. And then I ran across a teacher a number of years ago who made something astonishingly clear to me. She said, "Consider the possibility that your biggest faults are your grandest assets, simply with the volume turned up just a tiny bit too high. Consider the possibility that the very thing people fell in love with you because of, is what sometimes turns them away from you as well, because you've tweaked the volume just a little bit. And so, what maybe your friends call your unbearable braggadocio, when they say, 'He's just too too much,' is the same thing, the exact same quality, they look for, when it's 'Who can lead the pack? Who can get us out of this mess? Neale's the leader in the room. He's the one. That's why we like you so much, Neale.'"

I'm a very spontaneous person, so when people want somebody spontaneous who can dream up something just that quickly and pop it into the room just that fast . . . "Hey, Neale's the one."

That's also the part of me they say is (altogether now) "irresponsible." So, my irresponsibility is just my spontaneity turned up just one or two notches too loud. And so, what this teacher said was: "Neale, it's just a question of the volume sometimes being just a little bit off. But don't erase that. Don't try to change that about yourself. Don't try to eliminate that aspect of Who You Are from your behavior. Don't disown that. Just turn the volume down, ever so little, and notice that there's an appropriate volume to the aspects of Who You Are that renders itself acceptable in every moment. And sometimes you'll have to turn that volume up, and sometimes you'll have to turn that volume down."

Isn't that a delicious way to think of it? So now I don't have to think that I'm this person with all these faults. I simply have all these great qualities, sometimes turned up a little bit too much. (But not often—anymore.) Got it?

So, true relationships see and know all of this. True relationships are *foundationed,* or built upon, an entirely new paradigm that says: "I see in you what I choose to see in me. I give to you what I choose, myself, to receive." And true relationship also says: "What I take from you, or seek to disallow you to have, I take from me. I cannot allow myself to have what I will not allow you to have."

And so our challenge is: Can we live in a relationship without condition? Can we live in a relationship that doesn't ever say no, but simply says yes to another person? Can we use our relationships as an expression of the grandest kind of love we could ever imagine? Do we love our loved one enough to say the three magic words? Not *I love you*. They're, quite frankly, a bit overused. But here are the three magic words of every relationship: *as you wish.*

As *you* wish.

When we're prepared to say that, then we have truly given people back to themselves. Until we're ready to say that, we have simply sought to use our relationship with another to bring to us what we imagine ourselves to need in order to be happy. You have a question . . . .

Well, there are, you know, a million questions. But this is a subject that I have made my life about. I have been teaching courses on relationships for many years now. I'm in a long-term marriage. I have lived what you're speaking successfully for many years. And in the moment, I am not living it successfully. So, I would say that I've really done laps with this.

And I have a marriage that has enormous freedom in it. And it has been a marriage that's been grounded on a declaration I made when I began it, which was: our relationship works; it makes a difference, and everything contributes. So, I lived from the space that whatever was happening didn't need to match my pictures; anything that was going on was a part of how it was serving me. And it was, in fact, working, even when it didn't look the way I wanted it to. I saw that my ability to work with the challenges of it was how I could contribute to the world.

So, what's the problem?

Well, the problem is that somehow we are stuck in a power struggle that we are not moving through. And I cannot see how to move through it. So, I don't know what to ask. I just know that I do deeply love my husband. He deeply loves me on an essence level . . . .

So, I understand that you're in this power struggle. Now, I want to say to you with regard to that, something that may sound a bit heartless almost. So what? Why is that not okay with you? Why is the condition called being in a power struggle not okay with you? What's not all right about that?

I am basing a lot of my current dissatisfaction on what I'm not getting from the relationship. So, that conversation about not wanting to get anything from the relationship and only looking at what I want to put into the relationship is the seed I'm walking away with so far this morning. I hear what you're saying. There is a lack of the experience of love in the relationship. On an essence level, there's deep love. And when we surrender, there are many times we will almost step outside of our human identities, be with each other, and I feel like we finally have gotten out of the boxing ring. We're like the two boxers—when they ring the bell, they hang on to each other. There's that moment of love, because we do love each other deeply. And I am his equal, and he is my equal. And so we are enormously equal in the power struggle, and it wipes you out. And when there's this moment of not being in that struggle, there's a recognition of partnership and love, and the transcendent bondedness that's there. And in the everyday process of living, we are hurting each other a lot.

Well, stop it.

How do I do that without just adapting to conditions that really don't work for me?

Don't adapt to conditions that are not working for you. Simply stop making an issue over the fact that you refuse to adapt. Just don't adapt. For instance, I'm going to use a simple example. Let's say that someone decides . . . Let's say that my partner decided to take up smoking. My wife currently doesn't smoke, and neither do I, but I'm going to use a real easy example we can all kind of just get.

Okay, that'd be great.

So, now my wife comes home with a package of cigarettes, and decides: "Oh . . . I thought I'd tell you. I'm going to smoke." Well, I might have a problem with that. Not a problem with my wife per se, because my wife is still my Beloved. But now she's My Wife the Smoker. And I might have difficulty adapting to that behavior.

Well, I can simply refuse to adapt to that behavior. But I can do so without making my wife wrong, without making an issue of the fact that I'm not adapting to the behavior, without causing my refusal to adapt to that behavior to come between us. I can simply say to my wife, "Gosh, I love you, now as I always have. And it doesn't work for me for you to smoke in my presence. So I'm going to leave the room now.

Enjoy your cigarette. Incidentally, since you insist on smoking in the house continually, I'll probably have to leave the house because I don't like to be in a home that's filled with cigarette smoke. And I love you. I love you as dearly as I ever did, and I'm leaving the house now. And I love you."

Now my wife might say, if she were not very evolved (which she is, but if she weren't), she might say: "You mean you're leaving the house just because I'm smoking? And you're trying to tell me you're not making me wrong." And I would say: "I understand that you may have the need to tell me that I am making you wrong, but I'm simply allowing myself to live my authentic truth. I love you, and I notice you're smoking now. And what works for me is to be in a home that's smoke-free. So if you continue to smoke in this home, I'm going to have to live somewhere else. And I'm going to have to love you from somewhere else."

Okay. I get that.

The issues over which people traditionally enter into power struggles generally have to do with issues of time and availability and the activities of the other. In other words, you're not spending enough time with me, or you're engaged in activities with which I disagree. And we are at struggle about those issues. Now, I'll give you an example of what that could look like in real life: Suddenly your spouse turns into a workaholic, and while he was spending a lot of time with you in the first three years of your marriage, suddenly he's spending less and less, and now you're seven or eight or ten years into it, and he's hardly spending any time with you at all. And you enter into a power struggle over this because you are trying to control his time.

And so you say to him: "You know, I want you home at least three weekends out of four. I don't want you on the road all the time, or always on location shooting some great big film or doing some great big project, or poring over your work, or handling whatever it is that you're doing. You're not paying any attention to me." You wouldn't say it in those exact words, perhaps—maybe some who are very, very frank would—but most people would couch it in different terms. They wouldn't just come right out and say, "The truth is, I want your attention. I want your time." And so, there's a power struggle.

Maybe the partner will try to make an uneasy bargain: "Okay, I'll only go out on the road one weekend a month, or two weekends a month." He'll strike an agreement, and then if he decides to spend three weekends in a particular month away, he starts feeling guilty, he starts feeling *controlled*, and resentment builds up, and pretty soon you have a power struggle: "What right do you have to tell me what to do with my time?"

I would never enter into that kind of a power struggle with my spouse. If my spouse were doing anything, anything at all, with which I disagreed, or which didn't work for me, I would simply say: "You know, you can do as you wish. And I have to tell you that it doesn't feel good over here for you to spend three weekends out of four away from me, and away from this home. And it's okay if you want to do that, but I want you to know what I'm going to do if you continue that over a long period. I'm going to find someone else to spend my weekends with.

"That isn't a threat. I'm not trying to hammer you with this. It's simply an announcement of what works for me. I'd like to be with someone. I like to share the days and times of my life with a beloved other, and it's all right if you don't choose to be that beloved other. And so, you just do as you wish and as you please. And, no resentment, there's no anger, there's no upset, there's no make-wrong. Just a simple statement of fact. Now let me close my discussion with you with the following statement of fact: if I could choose anyone to be my beloved other, it would be you. That's why I'm wearing this ring on my finger.

You don't have to make the same choice in this moment, but I want you to know that you are my first choice, but also that I *do have a second,* and a third, and a fourth."

Now, that's simply a transfer of information, and that transfer of information need not be done belligerently. It's not about Gotcha. It's just saying, "This is what is so. This is simply what's so. And I share it with you lovingly and openly and candidly, as people who say they are in love with each other ought to do. This is my open, candid truth. And that's what so about that. And now we all have the facts, and we all can make informed choices.

"What I'm saying is not that I have someone in the wings ready to jump in here if you make one minor misstep, so you'd better watch your p's and q's; but what I am saying here is, if in the long run you choose to exhibit a behavior that is not working for me, that is simply not functional in my life—oh and by the way if I should choose in the long run to repeatedly exhibit a behavior that's not functional in *yours*—that there are options. I'm not limited to simply responding to that behavior by accepting it. I don't have to do that. And I just want you to know openly and candidly that, should you choose over the long run to exhibit that behavior, I will probably have to make some adjustments in how I'm proceeding with my life. And those adjustments might, in fact, include inviting someone else to share with me many of the things that I had hoped I'd be sharing with you."

You see, there's no power struggle when there's no struggle over power. There's simply each person—or at least one of the two (because it takes two to tango)—there's simply each person removing themselves from the struggle, and returning to the place of their own power, by allowing themselves to be, do, and have what they choose, without making the other person wrong about it.

"Choose what you're choosing. Choose to smoke. Choose whatever you're choosing, and I'll choose what I'm choosing." Now that allows my partner to make a value judgment. Is smoking important enough to her to allow her relationship with me to be changed in such a way that I'm no longer in the room? Or, for that matter, no longer even sharing the same house? And she'll make that value judgment. She'll either continue to smoke and demonstrate that smoking is, in fact, important enough to her to allow her relationship with me to change in such a way, or she will stop smoking. She'll alter her behavior. Not because I'm making her, but because she has made a free-will, empowered choice to notice that she can control the outcomes of her life by controlling her behaviors. See the difference?

I got it. Thank you.

You're very welcome. But that's how love reacts. Love does not struggle with power. Ever.

Yes, another question . . .

Neale, what is your own greatest challenge in relationships?

My own greatest challenge in relationships is transparency—remaining visible. Even after a number of years now with the same wonderful mate, there's always that little moment of fear. What if she finds out about this? What if she finds out about that . . . she won't love me anymore; you know, if she knows that I took that five thousand and invested into a stock and I lost it, and I never told her about that; or that I actually went out one afternoon and bought a car.

That was the big thing I did a few years ago in a previous relationship. I was driving down the road and I turned into a car lot—a new car lot. And I saw a car that I really, really wanted. And I said, "I'll take it." Just like that, I bought a car in twenty minutes. And I just drove it home. And then I thought all the way home, "This is ridiculous." I'm driving home thinking, "How can I hide this car from my wife?" I knew she had to find out sooner or later. Probably before dinner; you know, "Whose car is in the driveway?" But I actually was thinking (I went back to the sixth grade), "How can I prolong her knowing?" Then I thought, "You know, this is crazy." I got on the cell phone while I was driving and said, "Be outside when I pull up, I've got something to show you." And she said, "What are you talking about?" And I said, "I just bought a car." (Gulp)

So I think transparency is my greatest challenge in relationships, even with somebody whom I trust with my life. I mean, I really trust my wife with my life. I trust the unconditionality of her love. And still I worry about being totally clear and totally open and completely honest with her about every feeling, every thought, every idea, every understanding and misunderstanding, and every single thing that I'm doing, you know? And I'll tell you where that comes from, I think. I think my fear of transparency in relationships goes back to an age-old, ancient fear of God. Of course my idea was that God is going to "get me" for this.

By the way, I should tell you I still have that idea to this very day. At some small level, there's still a tiny part of my being—in spite of what's come through me, in spite of what's been written in the astonishing *Conversations with God* books—there are still some nights I roll around on the pillow, "Oh, man, what if I'm making this all up? I mean, what if I'm wrong about all of this? What if I've misled millions of people—about God? Boy, if I'm wrong, God is gonna get me good."

Then I have to become transparent with God, and say: "You know God, if I am wrong, I trust you'll know I didn't mean it. I mean, I didn't mean to intentionally mislead anyone. And if there's a shred of mercy left in You, gimme a break on this one."

You understand? Now that isn't at all the God that I know really exists. That's the God of my imagination, the God of my fear. And I think that the deep fear we have that we're going to be judged and misunderstood and punished by Deity is transferred to other people in our lives: to our spouse, to our loved ones, to our boss at work, to people who hold some place of importance in our life. And so, my biggest challenge in relationship is to think of those people who are important to me in relationship as I now want to think of God: as my best friend. I want to have a friendship with God, and I want to have a friendship with my spouse and all of my loved ones, of such quality that I can stand naked before them, mentally as well as physically, and say: "This is it—there's nothing hidden, there are no hidden agendas. This is *all* of it." That's my biggest challenge, and I face that challenge every day.

I want to ask you, just briefly, Neale, about mirroring in relationships—that what you dislike in the person you're with, you actually dislike in yourself. Could you just comment briefly on that?

You know, I don't dislike very much in other people anymore, because I learned long ago that what I saw over there that I disliked was merely something that I saw over here that I disliked. And in recent years I've come to like just about everything about me. Isn't that amazing? I mean, it's kind of hard to believe when you sit here and look at me, I suppose, but I really like so much about me now. I like my appearance. I like my attitudes. I like my ideas. I like my wackiness. I like my spontaneity. I like the part of me that's totally unconventional. I like the part that's not okay. You know, I even like my laugh. I mean, I like everything about me, and I have to tell you it's the first time in my life that I have felt that way. And because I feel that way, there's very little about other people now that I don't like. I've become tremendously tolerant. It's extraordinary that I look at people all around me, and I just love them all. I find acceptable, behaviors and characteristics and personality traits that even a few years ago I would have rejected out of hand. So I think that what happens is that with self-love comes an enormous love for other people, because I have to think to myself, "Gosh, you know, if you can love yourself, you can love anything."

What are the five levels of truth telling?

When I talk about transparency in relationships, I often think of telling the truth, which is what transparency really is all about. And I've been made aware that there are really five levels of truth telling.

The first level of truth telling is when you tell the truth to yourself about yourself. That was an enormous challenge for me, because I had been lying to myself for many, many years. It's hard to think of a person literally lying to themselves, but it's easy to do, and I did it for a long time.

The second level of truth telling is when you tell the truth to yourself about another. And I lied to myself about those kinds of things, as well, for many, many years. For instance, as an example, for years I told myself that I loved, in a romantic way, a person that I was with. Whenever I thought that I didn't, whenever I allowed myself to even imagine, "You know, maybe I'm not in love with her anymore," a voice inside my head said, "Don't be silly, of course you love her." Because that's what I was *supposed* to be thinking. That's how it was *supposed* to be for me. And so, I just lied to myself about that for the longest time, until one day I told the truth to myself about another. Didn't even utter it out loud, just told it to myself, which was a huge hurdle.

Then the third level of truth telling is when I tell the truth about myself *to* another, much as I'm doing with you right now.

And the fourth level of truth telling is when I tell the truth about another, *to that other*—my truth, of course, not *the* truth. *The* truth, objectively, doesn't exist, but I share my innermost truth about another, with that other.

And the fifth level of truth telling, when you get there, is when you tell the truth to everyone about everything. And if you can take these five steps, you've taken five steps to Heaven, because Heaven [pause] is not having to lie anymore.

I've heard it said that sometimes it seems that pain makes the heart break open so that it can experience more love. Why do our hearts sometimes need to be broken open in order to feel?

I don't think they do. Whoever said that pain makes the heart break open so it can experience more love maybe described a phenomenon that happens, but not one that *has* to happen. I think it's entirely possible to experience and feel more love without any pain at all. But we live our own cultural myth. There's a huge cultural myth out there that says that love hurts and that pain is the avenue; you know, no pain, no gain, that whole thing. I have to tell you I'm discovering and have been discovering now for the past several years, that it's possible to love joyously, and to feel all the love that the human heart can hold and more, without any pain whatsoever. So I'm ready now to say that I can reject out of hand the notion that pain and love have to go hand in hand, and that there's only one way to get from here to there, and that's through the doorway marked Pain. It's not necessary; it is a cultural myth, and we can step aside from it quite arbitrarily by simply choosing to do so.

So even when your lover leaves you, there's no pain?

There would be no pain when my lover left me if I've discovered the beauty and the wonder of who I am. I thought in the old days when my lover left me that my validation and my idea about who I am was walking out the door with her. I've now learned, and this is going to sound, I suppose in some ways, a bit crass, but it's the truth: when she walks out the door, I'll be okay. That's because I'm magnificent.

What role does your wife play in your career?

I'm going to give you an answer that's like a Divine Dichotomy. She plays every role and she plays no role at all. In other words, I'm very clear that my wife is not the force in my life that makes my career possible. If I thought that that were true, I'd be back into fear, that if I lost her, all would be lost. So I don't see my life partner as being that element which makes my life, as it's now being lived, possible. And yet, in some very mysterious and interesting way, without her, it wouldn't be possible. So it's a Divine Dichotomy.

The role that she plays in my life, I guess, is that my wife is the chief person in my life who sees me as I see me. She sees me as I imagine myself to be. Love does that. Love says, "I'm willing to see you as you see you in your best version of yourself. And that's how I'm willing to see you." In fact, love says more; love says, "Not only am I willing to see you as you see you in your best version of yourself, I'm willing to see you even as you don't see yourself. I'm willing to see you as more than you see yourself."

Someone once said, "If we saw ourselves as God sees us, we'd smile a lot." I think that my wife sees me as God sees me. She says things to me all the time, little things. My wife often tells me how handsome she finds me. You know, I shouldn't tell those tales out of school, I guess, but if I have a thought even for a moment that maybe it's not true, maybe I want to fall back to my prior thoughts about myself, that I'm not physically attractive, people like my wife, those who really love you, keep you affirmed in your most daring thoughts about yourself.

That's it! That just came through. People who *really* love you keep you affirmed in your most *daring* thoughts about yourself. You *are* it. You *can* do it. You know . . . those daring thoughts that we have in the middle of the night that we don't dare share with anyone else, because they're going to call us this, that, or the other—egotistical, or irresponsible, or whatever they're going to call us—if we let them hear those daring middle-of-the-night thoughts that we have about ourselves. Dare I think this about me? You know, when you're around someone who loves you deeply, you don't have to think these thoughts; they say them for you: "You are the best lover," "I have never known anyone so generous," "you are the kindest, most patient man I know," "you are an incredible person, and you are changing the world." My wife says those kinds of things to me all the time, every day. What role does that play in my life? I don't have words for that.

In the book, they talk about finding out what you want—what you want to be, what you want to have, and what you want to do. And in terms of relationships, I've taken that literally—by literally writing down the kind of partner that I would like to have. And I found that partners are showing up in ways that weren't the package I thought would show up. And it's kind of confusing, because I'm not sure, you know, whether I should just not sit down and write that out, and look at that as sort of like whatever the universe gives me. And I'd like to ask you to comment on that.

Sure. Thank you. It's a very good question.

With regard to relationships or anything else in life, I like to get very specific about what it is that I would choose. And after I've allowed myself to be very, very specific, *I take what shows up.* And the reason that I do that is that I never stop God from performing the miracles that She devises. And I never try to tell God what something should specifically look like, but merely what my idea about it is, in the moment.

You know, when I was a young man I had an idea of what the perfect mate looked like. And anyone who did not fit that mold was almost automatically rejected. I mean, I'd literally walk right past them, actually, and pay them no mind, almost as if they weren't there.

I'd go to a party. If it didn't feel a certain way, I'd leave because it wasn't what I'd expected. I was living my whole life out of my expectations, and most importantly, my relationships with people. And I was really missing such a huge part of it.

Some people may not fit any of your prior pictures of the kind of partner you thought you would wind up being involved with over the long run, for a whole variety of reasons. Maybe they are more sensible and not nearly as spontaneous as you are to give you just an example of what I'm talking about, and many, many other things as well. I now see that these differences need not create gulfs, nor are they necessarily items that render a potential partner "ineligible." Maybe they are, in fact, aspects of another's being that provide a perfect balance to who you are. I would never have seen that in my more immature days, however.

So my best advice to anyone who is seeking a mate, or really looking for anything in life, actually, is to have some idea of what you're looking for, for sure. But notice that sometimes goodness will come to you in packages that are quite unexpected, do not disallow, or render ineligible, those incoming energies. Because you're liable to find that what you're looking for is right under your nose, and you haven't seen it because your eyes weren't open.

Some of the most wonderful parts of my life have come to me in packages that are most unexpected and would have been called unacceptable just a few years ago. I mean—let me give you a silly example—I eat foods now that I would have called unacceptable even a few years ago. You know what I'm saying? I eat stuff now, and I'm open to it. My mother used to say, "Try it, try it." I never understood the wisdom of that. It's not only wise with regard to food, but with regard to everything in life. For heaven's sake, try it. I mean literally, for *Heaven's* sake. Because you might find your own Heaven right there. And so, don't get too tied in. And don't get too caught up in your expectations, but leave yourself wide open. And give God some room to create perfection for you.

What I've noticed in my life—I want to add to what this gentleman just said—is when I used to think I knew who I was looking for and all the qualities, I found that it was these qualities that I thought would make me, or make the relationship, feel a certain way. And then I discovered that, when somebody showed up and the feeling matched what I was trying to get from the package, that was the real value. And it didn't really matter the descriptions of the qualities, just that the feelings matched.

Yes, that's a very, very insightful and intuitive observation. And I want to share with the room that, while, in my life, I have tried to be as specific as I can with regard to what I want to show up—whether it's a job, or a person, or a new car—in my later years, as I've gotten a bit older, I learned to just drop all of those specific requirements. I've learned to really let go and let God. And I've learned to just notice that miracles come almost inevitably in packages that look quite unlike what I thought the package should look like. And so, I've kind of let go . . . . That's called living your life without expectation.

I think it's important to understand that love is a decision, it's not a reaction. Most people think that love is a reaction. I mean, that's really the main difference between the time when I lived out of expectations and had a certain package in mind, and when I dropped my expectations and found myself relating to people in a whole different way. The difference is that I've learned that love is a decision. You decide to love someone, or you decide not to, and it's really very, very arbitrary. Now one could say, "Yes, of course, but those decisions are based on appearance or personality, and so forth."

But I suggest that they sometimes are not. I suggest that they're sometimes based on something more arbitrary than that: a simple choice. I choose to love you. And when I really love you and come from a love that's pure, not only is my choice arbitrary, but it's unconditional. My love is unconditional. It's not conditioned on how your personality is showing up in this hour, or the shape and form of your body, or the size of your billfold, or anything else that's attendant to you. But, in fact, it does not know condition.

So when we choose to love someone, we are often in for a big surprise. We discover that the feeling we had hoped to get from being in love with the other person is really generated *over here*, and simply comes *to* us, *from* us, around that other person, almost like a planet flies around a sun, and then comes back to the other side in the heavens. It's that boomerang effect. And the great illusion is broken, at last. The illusion being, of course, that the feeling, that feeling of magic and wonderment, and that specialness, that I'm looking for in relationship, is coming from the other person. In truth, it was always coming from here. And when I send it there, and do so quite deliberately, it has no choice but to come back over here. It's like that song, "Return to Sender."

In the days when I wanted things or people or stuff to show up in a particular form, I had to ask myself the question that you're driving at, of course. Why do I have an idea that

that form is somehow better than another form? Why do I have an idea that thin is better than fat, or fat is better than thin, or black is better than white, or . . . What's my thought about that? What's that about?

As soon as I was willing to address that question, I could see that I was *making it all up.* I was just making all that stuff up. And suddenly I found it possible, when I let go of the things I was making up, to find treasures everywhere: in people that I never thought I could relate to, in things that I never thought I could find a love for. It's like a grown-up discovering that spinach isn't so bad after all.

You know, I've actually discovered that broccoli is an acquired taste. It's now really quite good. So you never know when broccoli will walk through the door.

Are there any other questions in the room about relationships? You all have it pretty well solved, do you? So, how many of you are ready to live in your relationship in a way that says, "My will for you is your will for you?" How many of you are ready to live in a relationship in a way that says to your loved one, "Love never says no?" [Hands go up]

That's great. Almost everyone in the room. Some hands go up just a little more slowly than others. But that's terrific. But please understand that this will not guarantee that the relationship will stay the way it now is. So, don't leave the room, thinking: "I've now just gotten the key. I'm going to live this way. And now my relationship will stay the way it is forevermore." The other person might, in fact, say: "Oh, thank you. Your will for me is my will for me? I'm out of here. My will for me has been to leave here for four years. I've just been waiting for permission." Kind of like, you know, getting out with honor.

So, I don't want anyone to think that what I'm suggesting is that by living this way, you'll somehow find the guarantee; we've all been trying to find that guarantee. "How can I make it work now and forevermore?" Well, you can't make it work now and forevermore. Or, more correctly, it *will* work, even forevermore, but the way it's working *may be different from the way you think it's supposed to work.*

One relationship that I was in ended, and I called it a tragedy when it ended—my God, I couldn't believe it—because it looked like it wasn't working. And the truth is that it was the ending of that relationship which opened the door to something much more enriching, and much more rewarding, in my life than I ever imagined I could experience. But it was only by allowing that which was going on to go on, and not judge it and make it wrong, and call it a tragedy, but just to simply let it happen, that I was able to experience what was coming to me next. So, I have discovered in my life that the universe works in extraordinary ways, and that if I just don't judge it, and allow it to do what it's doing, and to be what it's being, then I will find the peace and the joy that always resides within me.

And by the way, I want to say again, that's the largest key, if there is a key: I must stop looking to another for the peace and joy for which I have so long searched, and realize that that for which I have searched resides within me. My grandest joy and my greatest peace is experienced when I provide for another; in those moments, I am unlocking the greatest mystery and the greatest secret of all time.

And again I say, as I said before, here is the grandest irony: That in the moment that I see myself as the Source of that which I would receive from another, and in the moment when I choose to use my life to source that to another, in that moment I come as close to guaranteeing that the room will not empty out as I could possibly ever get. Because nobody leaves the room in which there resides the Source, or very few. And those who do? Let 'em go. Let them walk their path. Let them do what they're doing.

I'd like to go back to the matter of marriage. I've been thinking a lot lately, Neale, about the whole institution of the couple. And I'm very interested by what Book 3 said. Does marriage, as we have created it, call forth that kind of loving that we want? It seems to me that as we move more deeply into the twenty-first century, we're in a different place than human beings have ever been with regard to love and romance. Which is that we don't have to have it be about survival and procreation, which is what we've been up to since the beginning. So, I'm interested in knowing about forms other than the traditional form of the couple in marriage, such as living together, either with or without children, shared survival, that whole form. Are there other forms that we could begin to create that call forth that freedom and commitment, and the best in our loving?

That's a wonderful question. And the answer is: yes, there are many other forms now that stand aside from the traditional two-person relationship. We're seeing now intentional communities, in which a large number of people live together in a caring, sharing, and loving way. We're seeing what is loosely called—I know this is a bad word in some places—group marriages, or expanded or extended families, in which people are living together in caring, sharing, and loving ways.

We're seeing same-gender couplings in which people are living together in caring and sharing ways. By the way, if we don't stop making these paradigms wrong, we will never realize our richest and fullest potential as human beings. What happened to Matthew Shepard on that fence in Wyoming cannot and should never happen amongst beings who call themselves socialized and civilized, no matter what their beliefs. It's incomprehensible to me that that kind of behavior could occur, much less be condoned, by even a small portion of society.

I think that couples will always be here. And if you were to ask me if couples will continue to be the primary form of relationship, I believe they will. Always. There's something unique to that circumstance that really can't be re-created in any other form. So I think that always and forever, we'll see two people joining together and co-creating a life, and that will continue to be the primary form of loving human relationship. But, I think we will also see some other forms being created, and those forms will include extended families. They'll include group marriages. They'll include intentional communities. They'll include a variety of ways that people will gather together in numbers large and small to experience the one experience for which we all yearn: the experience of unlimited, unbridled love, one for the other.

We have been experimenting with those kinds of forms for a long time on this planet. And I think we'll see some of those experiments gain more respectability as people let go of their need to make them wrong. And I think that will happen here as we move into the next century.

The decision to stop making each other wrong for what we're doing is going to be a huge turning point in our social evolution. And that's going to happen here in the next ten to fifteen years—I'm very clear about that. We're going to stop making each other wrong for our sexual lifestyle choices. We're going to stop making each other wrong for our spiritual and philosophical choices. We're going to stop making each other wrong for our political and social choices. We're going to stop making each other wrong for our economic choices. We're going to stop making each other wrong, and simply say, at last, "Can't we just agree that we disagree?"

We're going to stop making each other wrong out of our awareness that making each other wrong is what's killing us, not the points of view that differ, but the fact that we are intolerant of them. Intolerance has seen its final day on this planet.

And we're going to see an evaporation of that intolerance, I think, in the years just ahead, to a large degree.

That will happen as a result of the evolution of the species that's being produced by these experimental ways that we are being together, and these new relationships that we are forming. And these relationships will permeate all of society. There will be new relationships in politics, in economics, in religion, new relationships at every level, and of course, new romantic relationships, as well. So, it'll be nothing to see a man and two women walking down the street, or a woman and two men walking down the street, in what's called a triad relationship, and they're holding hands and walking side by side, and enjoying the hell out of each other. I mean, enjoying the *Hell* right *out* of each other.

God says there is no form in which the expression of love which is pure and true is inappropriate. And the way we know that the expression of love is pure and true is that it never seeks nor allows itself to produce damage to another. I put that in the room because there's always somebody from the media, you know, from the far right who says to me: "He's just, he's just . . . giving a lot of people a license to do *anything* . . . he's condoning pedophiles." There's always someone who wants to go to an extreme to make me wrong. And what I'm saying is that there is no form in which a love which is true and pure is inappropriate. And love which is true and pure would not allow itself to damage another, or to take advantage of another, or to be abusive to another in any way.

And so, yes, the ways in which we will join with each other in the expression of our grandest idea of love are changing. People who think that the old way was the only appropriate way are having a difficult time with this. And some of them are gritting their teeth, and some of them are making wrong all of these other forms.

You know, there was a time when we were told, and we were seriously told—it wasn't somebody's whacko, way-out idea, but it was seriously held by the largest number of people in our society—that to couple with a person of another *race* was inappropriate. There were times when we were told that to marry and love another of a different *religion* was inappropriate. There are still people in certain races and religions who disown their loved one because their loved one loves another who is not "one of their own." How could we be not one of our own? There's *only one of us*. It's called the Human Family.

Our job as creators of the new society is to put in place a paradigm, a system, if you please, a new social, and spiritual, and political (because much of this is about politics) construction that allows us to simply love each other in a way that feels pure inside of our soul, regardless of gender, or color, or religion, or any other artificially restrictive factor. How can it be wrong to love each other? How can there be a wrong way to express pure love which would never damage or hurt another? Yet, our uptightness about that, based on what we, in our arrogance, presume to be the Will of God . . . I mean, can you imagine a time, and we're not talking about centuries ago here, but a couple of generations back, when we actually stood up and seriously suggested that it was God's law that we should not marry interracially? That it violated the law of God? Help me out. And we actually believed that.

In fact, there are people who still believe it today. I know a Jewish couple who disowned their son for marrying a non-Jew. What's the word they use for it? Gentile, goyim. And they've disowned him because he married outside the faith. What is that? That is a thought that says not only am I separate from you—which is a false-enough thought—not only am I separate from you, but guess what? I'm better than you. We're better than they are. So how could you possibly marry *that?* Those are the kinds of thoughts that have created the kinds of miseries that have been visited upon this planet for lo these many years.

Yet, it is the new understandings that you bring into the new days and times into which we all are now ushering ourselves, that will create a new experience. The world, with regard to the subject we call love, has been waiting for a long time for a savior to come again. That savior has already arrived. She sits right there, and there [pointing to members of the audience]. And he's right there, and he's there.

Will you save us from our lowest idea about ourselves? And will you take us to our grandest place? We can only go as high as you're willing to go. We can only become as extraordinary as you're willing to be. We can only love as fully as you're willing to love. You're it. You're the one. There are those who see the world as it is, and ask, "Why?" And those that see the world as it could be, and ask, "Why not?" Thanks for listening.

Part Two

Relating to Oneself and One's Personal Experience

Introduction

Of course, we cannot relate to others in any meaningful way unless and until we relate to ourselves and to our own daily experience in a way which reflects the Truth of Who We Are. There are many things that all of us want—yet the greatest irony of life is that what all of us want, all of us have.

We have an abundance of that which we wish we had an abundance of.

You may not believe that this is true for you, or for others that you observe or know, but it *is* true, and it is only our thought about it *not* being true that makes it not *seem* true in our experience.

Perspective plays an extraordinary role in how we experience life. What one person calls Lack, another person calls

Plenty. And so, our private definitions create our private experiences. And our definitions, or what I call our decisions about things, duplicate and enlarge themselves. What we say is so is what will grow to be so.

How do I know? Because I'm a good listener. You see, like the other topics I am covering in this book, I've been asking questions about abundance, abundant living, money, and this thing that some people call right livelihood for some time.

What I have learned for these many years of exploration—and from my *Conversations with God* experience, is that most of us do not understand what abundance really is, confusing it with money. Yet when we take stock of that in which we truly are abundant and choose to share it freely with everyone whose life we touch, we find that what we *thought* was abundance (money) is the smallest part of it; and that financial stability (and even wealth) comes to us much more freely than we imagine—as do all the wonderful gifts of God.

Many of us cannot accept this, however, because when we think of money, we imagine that it is an experience and an energy that stands outside of the reality of God. Some people have this so confused that they believe that *good things* should come for free—or at least at a very low cost. So we pay our nurses and our teachers and our ministers and our *at-home parents* the smallest amount (if, in the last example, *anything at all*) for the services they render, while we toss hundreds of millions at football players and film stars and the people who sit in enormous offices atop high buildings in the corporate centers of our world.

Yet once we understand that money is a part of what God *is,* our attitude about it changes. We see it as an extension of the glory of God, not the root of all evil. There is nothing in the universe that stands outside of the glory of God—that is not a *part* of God. This awareness can produce astonishing results insofar as money is concerned.

It *is* possible to experience abundance, and the extraordinary insights in the *Conversations with God* books show us how. So here are those insights, as I have received them, understood them, and shared them in this second portion of a televised interaction that I had with a live studio audience exploring this topic with me.

Well, nice to see you all here. Good morning, everybody.

Well, I suppose you wonder why I called this meeting. And so do I. I'd like to start off our time together this morning just chatting a little bit about what happened to me in my life. I wanted to kind of roll into some of the experiences that I've had over the last six or eight years, bring you up to speed and up to date, and let you know what that was like for me. And we can go from there, and begin talking about the specific topics that I hope we have a chance to explore here together.

How nice of you to choose to be in the room with me on this day. And how nice of you to choose to be on the planet with me at this time. This is a very, very important time. People have said that for centuries, and they've always meant it. But I'm not sure it's always been quite as true as it is right now.

We're moving into a period of time on this planet when the decisions and choices we make will produce a critical impact and an extraordinary effect on the lives that we are collectively creating. So, it's really important that we come together in groups like this, groups large and small, and share our reality, share our understanding, become even more clear about what it is that we hold in common. And when we find that there are differences between us, find a way to celebrate those differences. Because if we don't learn how to celebrate our differences, we're not going to be able to make a difference on this planet. And you came here to make a difference. That's why you came to this body, at this time. That's why you came to this particular planet at this particular moment. Whether you know it or not, you came here with a very big agenda. And for most people, if you're like me, the agenda is much larger than you might originally have thought or imagined. I'm going to repeat that. I said: for most people, if you're like me, the agenda is much larger than you might originally have thought or imagined.

To begin with, your life has nothing to do with you. And that might change your whole idea about what you're doing here. And your life has nothing to do with your body. That also might change your whole idea about what you're doing here. Your life has to do with the agenda that has been set for you by you, by that part of you that we've come to call, in our language, your soul.

And it has been my observation that very few people have spent a lot of time during this particular life paying attention to the agenda of their soul. I know that I haven't. Most of my life, I paid attention to the agenda of my ego, of my mind, of my body—in other words, of that part of me that I thought that I really was. And I paid very little attention to the agenda of my soul, to the real reason that I'm here. And yet, those of us who begin to pay attention to the real reason that we're here begin to make an extraordinary impact on the world—an impact beyond anything that you might have imagined possible. Suddenly you find yourself at a—at a precipice, at the edge. And it is very much, as Apollinaire once put it, "Come to the edge."

"We can't. We're afraid."

"Come to the edge."

"We can't. We'll fall."

"Come to the edge." And they came. And he *pushed* them. And they flew.

There are a few of us, a very few of us, who are now ready to fly, who are ready to go, as Gene [Roddenberry] said, to places where no human has gone before—who are really ready to fly now, and to take all those whose lives they touch with them, on a flight of fancy that will truly change the world. And in these days and times, you will have an opportunity to decide whether you are one of those select few—selected, I might add, by yourself, not by anyone else. This is a self-selecting process. You'll wake up one day and look in the mirror, and say, "I select me. I choose me. I'm it." It's a game of tag, with only one player. "I'm it."

It is very much *like* a children's game, you know. It is very much like a children's game, played with the abandon and with the joy of children who play together—except in this game, there is only one player. And now you get to quit playing hide and seek, and you get to start playing tag. "I'm it." "You're it." "Thank you very much."

So, in these days and times, you get to choose yourself; or not, as you wish. As *you* wish. But if you choose yourself to play in this particular game, you'll find that you have caused yourself to set aside all of your prior beliefs, understandings, thoughts, and ideas about what it is that you are doing here, about why you brought yourself to your body at this time and in this place. You'll change everything you ever thought about that. And you'll find that your life, indeed, will have nothing to do with you, or with your body.

And yet the irony is that, in the moment that you decide and declare that your life has nothing to do with you or your body, everything you ever sought, hungered for, struggled to obtain for yourself and for your body will come to you *automatically*. And you won't even care. Because you will no longer need it. You will enjoy it, for sure. But you will no longer need it. And the struggle will at last be over.

But it will have just begun for the hundreds and the thousands and, maybe, the millions of people whose lives you will touch. And you will see them every day—people for whom the struggle really has just begun, who are taking those first few steps on the journey home. And they, like you, will reach out a hand, figuratively, if not literally, and sometimes even quite literally. And they'll look around them and hope to find someone who will reach a hand back, who will say, "Come, follow me," who will *dare* to say, "I am the way, and the life. Follow me."

That may sound almost too religious for some people. But this is the third and the last of the children's games that the child in us, which is our soul, will play. No longer Hide and Seek; no longer You're It; now, Follow the Leader.

Follow the leader. And you're the leader. And we're going to follow you. We're going to walk in your footsteps. I'm going to make the choices that you are going to make. We're going to make the decisions that you are making. We're going to say the words that you say, touch the world in the way that you touch it. We're going to follow your lead.

If you thought that the whole world was watching you this day, and following your example in everything that you think and say and do, would it change in any way how this day went for you? Maybe for some of you, just a little bit.

Well, the whole world is following you, whether you know it or not. That's the great secret: the whole world—surely the world whose lives you touch—is following you. We're watching you. We're seeing Who You Really Are. And we're seeing who you think that you are. And we're taking our cue from you. Like actors on a stage, we are imitating you, because we have no one else to imitate. We're all that there is. There's no one else.

We can look outside of ourselves for some larger example out in the sky someplace—maybe even in our imaginations. But in the end, we will imitate each other. In the end, children will imitate their parents, and parents will imitate their parents. And nation will imitate nation. In the end, we will take our cues from each other, until one of us steps out and says, "Not that way. This way."

So your decision at this time in your life, at this really critical period as we transition into what is truly a new age, your decision is critical. It's not a small decision. Because you're not making it just for you. The decision you make in these days and times, you're making for everyone else in the room. And the reason for that is very clear. Because there *is* no one else in the room. Except you. Here you are, in your many other manifest forms; here you are. And so the decision you make for you, you make for all of us. Because there's only one of us here.

That might sound a little esoteric. First we sound religious, then we sound esoteric. But it is these thoughts, these concepts, these ideas which must begin to drive the engine of our collective human experience, or our collective human experience will not be collective much longer, but will, in fact, disintegrate and fall apart, even as will our planet.

We are at that point now. You know when airplanes in the old days used to cross the ocean, they called it the point of no return? Too far to turn back, not far enough to safely make it there? There's this little red zone, you know, when you're neither there nor here, you're neither here nor there.

It feels very much as if that's where we are right now on this planet, in many ways: in terms of our ecology, in terms of our worldwide economy. We see, in many areas of the world, the whole thing is falling apart, in terms of our social structures, our spiritual understandings, the education of our offspring. In so many ways and in so many areas, it feels as if we're in that no-man's land, in that red zone. We're not here, and we're not there, either. Neither here nor there, but we're beyond the point of no return. We have crossed the Rubicon.

I'm giving away my age with all of these phrases. Anyone under thirty-five is saying: "'Cross the Rubicon?' What the heck is that?"

We've crossed the Rubicon, and now the question is, what do we do, and how do we get the rest of us to go over to the other side. And the answer to that question will be, in fact, supplied to the human race by people like you. By you.

And if you think it's about people like me who happen, in this particular day and time, to be enjoying our fifteen minutes in the sun, you're wrong. I want to impress on you here today that it's not about the people in the front of the room. I just happen to be here now by—I want to say—by sheer happenstance. It could just as easily be you. As a matter of fact, one of you just come on up here and do the rest of the program [laughter]. Just a thought.

But that is the real test. That is the real question. How many of you, if given the opportunity, if called to the challenge, if selected, would say: "Hey, Neale, you know what? I'm ready! I'll take the chair, I'll take the place in the front of the room." Because the real secret of life is that you're in the front of the room anyway, whether you know it or not. That's the point I've been trying to make. You're in the front of the room anyway. It just looks as if you're not. In fact, the real irony of life is that there's no place *other* than the front of the room. There's no back of the room. So, you can't hide out anymore. So, Follow the Leader, it turns out, is mandatory.

Let me tell you how I wound up in this chair, just to give you a little bit of background on how all this began. In 1992, I had reached the end of the line for me. In 1992, I had reached a point where I was losing again another committed relationship with a significant other. My career had reached a dead end. My health was falling apart. Nothing was working in my life. And this relationship that I had with my significant other was the one that I knew would last forever. And there it was, in front of my face, just disintegrating right in my hands.

It wasn't the first time that such a relationship had disintegrated right in front of me. Nor was it the second. Nor was it the third, or the fourth. And so I [laughter] I knew that there was something I don't know here, that the knowing of which would change all of this for me—I didn't know what that was. And in my relationship life, I simply couldn't find that secret.

And then in my career, I was having the same kind of challenges. You know, I had read all the books: *Do What You Love, The Money Will Follow.* I don't think so—unless it does, of course. But I couldn't seem to find the formula. I was either doing something that I did love, but I was dead broke; or I was making enough money to skim by, making it through, but my soul was dying a thousand deaths. I didn't seem to know how to put the two together. Not for very long. If I did get it together, it was always for about six or eight months, then it would all fall apart. I couldn't seem to glue the pieces together and make them stick.

And likewise, my health: I couldn't seem to get through a year without something going on, and sometimes it was a pretty big thing that was going on. I mean, I had ulcers and I was thirty-six. I had lots of stuff happen: chronic heart problems, just a pile of stuff I'm not even telling you about. And so, at the age of fifty, I really felt as if I was eighty years old—and not a very healthy eighty years old at that: arthritis, fibromyalgia, just stuff going on. You know what I'm saying? I couldn't get this mechanism to work. All of this was happening at the same time.

Now, see, usually God had been better than that. It was usually one thing or the other in my life. But for this particular period, for reasons that still aren't clear to me, it was all at once, at the same time. "Oh," God said, "let's give him a triple whammy. Let's do the old career-relationship-body number in the same week." And so, there I was. It was kind of like a triple lutz, you know, kind of a metaphysical triple lutz. And I was skating on thin ice. I didn't know where to go with it. I was very, very, *very* angry—threatening to fall into chronic depression.

And one night I threw back the covers of the bed, because I had awakened in the middle of the night filled with rage and upset over how my life was. I stormed out into the larger part of the house, looking for answers in the middle of the night. I went to where I always go for answers in the middle of the night, but there was nothing decent in the refrigerator that night, so I went to the couch instead. And there I sat on the couch.

Try to picture that, sitting there in the middle of the night, four o'clock in the morning, on the couch, stewing in my own juice, as it were. Then I called out to God. I thought, "Well, I can run around and tear apart the house, break the dishes, or whatever." But I sat there and I called out, "God, what does it take? What does it take to make this game work? Somebody tell me the rules. I promise I'll play. Just give me the rules. And after you give them to me, don't change them." And I asked a ton of other questions as well.

And then I saw, on the coffee table in front of me, there happened to be a yellow legal pad lying there. There was a pen next to it. So I picked it up, flicked on a lamp, and I began to write my anger out, you know. Seemed to be a safe, quiet way to deal with it at four fifteen in the morning. I don't know how it is with you, when you are angry and when you're writing, but I write really big when I'm getting angry. And there I was. *What does it take?* I was really angry. *To make life work. And what have I done to deserve a life of such continuing struggle?* Exclamation point, exclamation point, exclamation point.

And on and on I went like that for about twenty minutes, just writing out my anger, you know, defying the universe to give me a response. And then I finally calmed myself down, just a bit, felt just a little bit better. And I felt okay. I thought, "Hey, that worked. I have to share this process with some friends. That works."

I fell asleep. Then I was awakened by a little voice, right over here, just over my right shoulder. I call it now my voiceless voice. When I first heard the voiceless voice, it was very much as if someone was whispering in my right ear. And the feeling that came over me was one of extreme calm. I was, I want to say, becalmed—very much at peace and filled with kind of an indescribable joy.

You know, I think of moments in my life when I've had that joy . . . like the moment when people marry—not even the whole ceremony, but that particular moment when the minister finally says, you know, "Do you . . . "And in that moment you look in the other's eyes and maybe just pause for a moment and then say, "I do." There is just that tiny sliver of a moment when your whole body is filled with something you can't describe, and you realize that you're making an enormously important decision, a huge choice, and that you're so glad about it that there's not even a tiny bit of doubt about it—that moment of total gladness . . . joy really.

I think all of us have had those moments, maybe three or four, perhaps five times in a lifetime, when we just are filled with that sense of rightness—this is totally right, this is totally joyful. That's how it felt in that moment when I first heard that voiceless voice. Just . . . joy. A peaceful, calming joy.

And the voiceless voice said, "Are you ready now?" And I woke up and listened more closely, and the voice said, "Neale, do you really want answers to all of these questions, or are you just venting?" I said, "Well, you know, I am venting, but if you have answers, I'd sure as heck like to know what they are." And with that the answers came—in a flood. The answer to every question I ever asked came to me. And so fast that I felt I had to write them down or I would forget them. You see, I never intended to write a book. I was simply writing this stuff down because I didn't want to forget all that was coming to me.

So I wrote it down in a flood, as fast as my hand could fly. And as I read what I was writing, it brought up, naturally, other questions for me. Because it was astonishing stuff that was coming off the pen. So, I started writing the questions that the answers brought up for me, and that brought more answers. And I wrote more questions, and that brought more answers. And before I knew it, I was involved in an on-paper dialogue with what I later came to know must be God.

That's the short story of how I happen to be here—and wound up sending that on-paper dialogue to a publisher. People ask me, "Why did you do that if you weren't intending to write a book?" And I thought, "Well, I'll just test God." I was actually testing Deity. Because when I wrote that out, *This will one day become a book,* my first idea was you and a hundred other people are going to send your middle-of-the-night mental meanderings to a publisher, who's going to jump on them immediately, and say, "My God, of course, *we'll publish this right away*"? And millions of people across the world are going to buy this thing.

Except that's, in fact, exactly what happened. And it was published. And millions of people have purchased it. It's been translated into twenty-seven languages around the world. It's really astonishing to see something you've written come out in Japanese or Greek or Hebrew, and to realize that, in fact, you've touched the entire world.

A Digression

Why am I sitting here in the front of the room? I want to tell you why I've chosen to be in the front of this room. I'm very clear now that I was called on to be a messenger. I'm very clear now that, in fact, I've always been a messenger, and that there's no place I can allow myself to be *except* in the front of the room. Because I have a very important message to share with everyone whose life I touch. And here is the important message

I've come to share: *All* of you are messengers, and there's no place else for you to be except in the front of the room. All of you have come to share a very important message with everyone whose life you touch. And here is the important message that you have come to share with them: All of them, each of them, is a messenger. And they have come here with a very important message to share. And there's no place else they can be except in the front of the room. And here is the important message they have come to share: Everyone is a messenger.

And it was a dark and stormy night, and a group of bandits was seated around the campfire. And one of the bandits happened to say, "Chief, tell us a story." And the chief said, "It was a dark and stormy night, and a group of bandits was seated around the campfire, when one of the bandits happened to say, 'Chief, tell us a story.' And the chief said, 'It was a dark and stormy night . . .'"

So, you see, it's circular. The eternal story of life is the same story. The glorious message I've come to share is the same message. The message is that you have come to share a message. And the message you've come to share is that they have to come to share a message, and here's the message all of us have come to share with each other: "Hello, *wake up*. Do you know Who You Really Are? Hello. *Wake up*. Do you understand?"

Here's the message we've come to share: You and I are one. There's only one of us in the room. If you think we're separate, cut it out. We're not separate. There's only one of us in the room. And there's no difference between us. And if you think there's a difference between us, cut it out. Because there is no difference between us. And stop trying to create an artificial difference where there is none. And when you can't, then you and I are one, and there's only one of us in the room, and only one of us on the planet, and only one of us in all of creation. Everything that causes you pain and misery, travail and struggle, heartache and difficulty, will disappear. It will simply go away.

So stop thinking that you're over there, and I'm over here. There's no place where you end and I begin—such a simple, elegant message that changes everything. When will we get it? *When will we get it?* We'll get it when we send it. Did you hear that? We'll get the message when we *send* the message.

So, here we are together today. I walked into the room and I thought, "What in the devil am I doing here? See, if I'm not careful, it's liable to look as if I have something to say that you don't know. I've got to be real careful about that. And if we're not careful, it could look to *you* as if you have something to hear that you don't know; that you've never heard before.

If we're not careful, we're liable to forget who we really are, and we're liable to play a game called I Know and You Don't." Except that I'm not willing to play that game, now or ever. I'm very clear that there's nothing I have to say that you don't already know. So, thanks for coming, and goodbye.

I've been trying to figure out some way to get out of the room since I walked in here. That'll work as good as any. All right, before we go any further, because we're going to talk here a little bit about one of our most important subjects, which is the subject of abundance and right livelihood . . . but before we do, somebody had their hand up. And I've been ignoring it for fifteen minutes.

When you described you heard the voice, the left part of your shoulder . . .

Actually, it was my right shoulder, but who's looking?

And subsequently, when writing, asking questions, writing books, getting a response, was there a particular feeling associated with that particular voice or that particular impulse to write, that authenticated it over, say, other times we hear a voice or other times we're urged to write? Was there something, something else, a presence or a feeling or . . . Can you describe that for us, what that felt like?

It was a softness. It felt as if my whole body had just turned into Jell-O. I almost don't know how to describe that. It was just a releasing of every bit of anxiety or tension, or I want to say, negativity, within me, as I sat on that couch. I can recall just—almost as if, without any act of volition on my part— I'm going to release my tension here. It just happened. I just suddenly . . . And then, from that softness sprang a . . . It's sort of difficult to discuss this. I go right back into it, almost immediately.

Almost feels like a peace descended?

It's a peace and a sense of comprehensible joy, and one- ness—a joy that almost brings tears. That kind of deep, deep joy. And from that first moment, I just sat there, and the tears began to flow. Before I wrote more than ten words, I can recall the experience of the ink blotching on the page. I was using one of those felt-tip pens—and the ink was running as my tears were flowing.

I've kind of gotten used to the experience now. So, I'm aware of what's going to happen. But I know what it feels like. Have any of you ever been present at the moment that a baby is being born? And held her in your hands for those first three or five minutes of her life? If you've ever had that experience, that's what it felt like. It felt that way, like when I held my child for the first few moments of her life and looked in her face. And there was no other feeling I could have, except one-ness, complete connectedness, love that knew no limitation of any kind, and no condition at all. Just a sense of . . . You can't even put it into words, that's how it felt—like holding your newborn child in your hands. That's how it felt. And I knew, in that moment, that I was, in fact, holding a newborn child in my hands. I knew that I had given birth to a new Me.

You know, I've never said that before. Just in answer to your question, that imagery comes up for me. You'll know when you're reborn. No one has to tell you when you've been born again. You will know it. And you'll come out of that moment never again feeling the same, ever—about yourself or anyone else.

All barriers between you and other people will drop away. All sense of separation will disappear. And then you'll become very dangerous. Because you'll want to walk up to people and give them great big hugs. You know, you'll want to just go to people and say, "I love you so much" [laughter] and hope they don't have you arrested . . . especially if, God forbid, you should do it to another man . . . because society says you're not supposed to do that to another man. If you're a man, be careful . . . same-gender stuff. You know, we have all of these . . .

Excuse me, I cry at my own material [laughter].

From the beginning of time, all we have ever wanted was to love and be loved. And from the beginning of time, all we've ever done is create moral restrictions, religious taboos, societal ethics, familial traditions, philosophical constructions, all manner of rules and regulations telling us who, when, where, what, and how we may love; and who, when, where, what, and how we may not. Unfortunately, the second list is longer than the first.

What are we doing? *What are we doing?* If I walk up to this guy, and I say, "The beauty of me sees the beauty of you," what is wrong with that? Or if I walk up to a stranger, and say, "I see who you are," how is that not okay?

I don't understand how we've decided to construct it here, people. But I've got to tell you this: If we don't change the construction, we will never have the truest experience of who we really are. So, it's time to rebuild and re-create. It's time, in fact, to re-create ourselves anew—in the next grandest version of the greatest vision we ever held about Who We Are.

Boy, oh boy, oh boy, oh boy . . . . Don't get me going. See, you put me in front of a room full of people like this, and I see new members of the army. What can I do to recruit them? How can I get them to play, you know? Did you ever have that feeling when you walked down to the playground? I used to walk over the hill to the playground in our neighborhood. We had a big playground about eight blocks from my house. And as I got closer, I'd get excited: "I wonder who's there. I wonder who's there." As I'd approach, I'd see some kids out there playing around. Some of them I'd recognize, some of them I didn't know, from some other part of the neighborhood. I can always remember thinking: "How can I get them to play with me?" Did you ever have that feeling when you approached the playground?

Then you'd get to the playground, and some kids would say: "Hey. Hi, Neale. I'll play with you." And other kids would go, "Oh, it's big mouth Walschie again." And you'd get rejected. Anybody here ever get rejected on the playground? None of you, huh? None of you are former playground rejectees? That's how it feels when I walk into a room like this. "Oh, boy, I wonder if they'll play with me. Wouldn't it be fun if they did?"

So, let's play around a little bit with this material. Let's take a look at some of the things that have been told to me in this extraordinary dialogue that I found myself engaged in. Let's talk about abundance.

Abundance is a topic in which I have had a great deal of interest through the years. And so have many people. And the first thing I came to understand about abundance was that, when I began to look at it deeply, and when I began to receive my information from a higher authority, I have been mis-defining what abundance really is. I thought that abundance was stuff, that it had to do with how much stuff I had.

I hate to be simplistic here. I hate to be really obvious with what I'm going to tell you, because I know you already know this. But for those of you who have forgotten that you know, I'd like to remind you of what I was reminded of in my dialogue: true abundance has nothing to do with anything that I am having, and everything to do with what I am being. And that when I share my abundance of beingness abundantly with all those whose lives I touch, everything I sought to have came to me automatically, without my even trying to have them.

All the stuff that I thought abundance was about: all the fine crystal, you know, and the wonderful antiques, and the beautiful clothes, and all that, just kind of fell into place without my struggling for it. So that I was seeking what I thought was abundance, and it was just stuff. And that which I already *had* a great abundance of, I was virtually ignoring.

I recall sitting in a room full of people, a little bit larger than this, not too many weeks ago, when I was facilitating a retreat in the beautiful mountains of Colorado, in Estes Park. And in that room, a person said to me, "I wish I could experience abundance." That was his issue. And he said: "You know, I don't make a great deal of money. I have barely enough to get by. I had to really squeeze pennies to get here." And so forth. And he said, "I've all my life wanted to experience the kind of abundance that I see you"—and he pointed to me in the front of the room—"experiencing." And I said, "Well, you know, if you really want to have the experience of abundance, why don't you spend your lunch hour giving abundantly of that which you have to give." And he looked at me, astonishingly enough, and he said, "I have nothing to give."

He really thought—he wasn't even making that up—he really thought he had nothing to give. And so I had to look at him and begin to say the obvious. "Do you have any love to give?"

"Oh," he said, and he wasn't even sure about that. But, I think, he had to concede the point that perhaps there was a morsel of love within him that he could give. He said, "Yeah, yeah, I suppose I have some love to give."

I said: "Do you have any compassion? Does compassion reside within you at any level?"

"Yeah, well, I suppose I have a little bit of compassion. People have called me a compassionate guy."

It was hard for him to say that, by the way. He was having a hard time saying the word *compassion* in the same sentence as the word me. But he allowed as to how, perhaps, he had some of that to give as well.

So, did he have any humor?

He said, "Oh, yeah . . . I got enough jokes to last for a lifetime."

I said, "Terrific."

We made a list of the things that he had in abundance. But, of course, he didn't think that had anything to do with abundance as he was describing it. I said: "Okay, let's agree that we disagree on our definitions of what abundance is. But let's agree that you do have an abundance of *these things*." We could agree on that.

I said: "Great. Now, here's what I want you to do. Spend your lunch hour, and I want you to give of these things that you have acknowledged that you do have in abundance. Give of them in profusion. Give more than you ever gave before, to everyone whose life you touch for the next ninety minutes while we're on our lunch break. That's my challenge to you." And he agreed to accept the challenge.

And so he went off on the lunch hour, which was just a few minutes from that time, and he began to outpour that of which he had abundantly, to everyone in this YMCA camp where we were doing this retreat . . . there was not just our group, but groups from other places that rented different lodges, so there were maybe six hundred people at this place; two hundred of them were in our retreat, and four hundred from other places. So, there were lots of strangers who didn't know who this guy was, or what he was up to. So, he walked into the cafeteria. It was like a major confrontation for him. Because it was like, my group knows that I'm going to act crazy now, but the rest of these people don't know that I'm now going to act kind of nuts.

You see, when you give of yourself abundantly, half the world calls that crazy. They say you must have something going on with you, something's wrong. People don't act that way. Which, of course, is the problem. People don't act that way. So, here he is, walking up to people in the cafeteria, and he is sharing, abundantly, of that which is abundantly his. He's sharing of his love, and his good cheer, and his humor. He was telling jokes all over the cafeteria. Some folks were laughing, "Ha ha ha ha, that's pretty funny." And other folks were laughing, "Ha ha . . . Who is this guy?" But everyone couldn't help but laugh a little. And those who didn't think his joke was that funny couldn't help but grin a bit at this wonderful guy, this "Santa" who just showed up in the cafeteria all of a sudden.

He was going around saying wonderful things to people. One person, it just happened, was not in that good of a mood, and it was his opportunity to show some compassion. And he showed compassion by not telling anymore of his bad jokes. That can be an act of compassion, I have learned. But then he sat down next to that person. He said: "I don't know you, but I'm from this other group that's doing a retreat in the other lodge. Everything okay?" Before he knew it, he had become involved in a conversation with God. And he got to express that part of himself.

This guy came back from the lunch hour, ninety minutes later, feeling so huge, feeling so big. And he said, "I can't tell you how I feel." I said, "Do you feel abundance now?" He said: "Yes, I do. I feel abundantly wealthy. With all these grand parts of me that I haven't really given myself permission to express. Hadn't given myself permission to do that."

But what was really funny, and here's the trick that the group played on him . . . while he was at lunch, somebody went to the room and got their hat, and everybody in the room put money in the hat. So, when he got back to the room, the guy had a lot of money in the hat. Because the room just wanted to prove to him, you know, what goes around, comes around, and all that. It was just this incredible in-the-moment experience of the truth. Did you ever have one of those in-the-moment experiences of the truth? You just go, "Bong!" Palm to forehead, "Duh." Because it's just so obvious, and so obviously expressed.

So, after he sat in his chair and told everyone about this, they handed him this pile of money. And he just sat there . . . the tears started to flow. And he had a direct experience of what is eternally so: that which you give to another, you give to yourself. And you can give it in one form, and it will come back in another. But it cannot fail to come back to you, because there's only one of us in the room. And his life changed out of his new awareness of what abundance truly is.

Even people living in the streets can develop a consciousness of abundance. First, they can do so by causing others to have that which they would choose to experience themselves. For as little as you have, you will find someone who has even less.

I'm reminded of the story of a guy named Joe who actually lived in San Francisco on the streets. And as little as he had, he made it his job every day to find someone who had less than he had. If he managed to panhandle a couple of bucks on the street, he'd give two and a half times that to someone who had even less. And he was a very abundant guy; he was known as the king of the streets, in fact, because he was the source of abundance for everyone else on the street.

People on the streets can begin to experience abundance if they are willing to allow someone else's life that they are touching to experience abundance in that moment. That might seem easier said than done—I mean, I'm sitting here in the lap of luxury making that statement. And I don't want to sound shallow. And I don't want to sound gratuitous. But I lived on the street. I lived on the street for nearly a year of my life. And I remember what pulled me out of it.

So, the first thing I want to share with you about abundance is: get clear what abundance is. And if and when you decide to give abundantly of the grandest part of Who You Are, with everyone whose life you touch, if you decide to do that, your life will change in ninety days. Maybe ninety minutes. Be careful. Because people will suddenly get who you are.

Let me explain to you the difference between lawyer A and lawyer B. See, here are two lawyers, and they both have an office on the same block, in the same city. They both graduated from the same college, and they both graduated at the top of their class. So, they have equal skill levels. It's not about location, because they're both on the same block, in the same city. Yet, one lawyer, lawyer A, is doing fabulously well. And lawyer B, just a few feet down the block, is not doing so well. What's that about? What's happening there? What causes one person to be the thing we call successful, and another person not, given everything else being equal? Just to set up the discussion.

So, it's not about, well, he was born into wealth, and he was born into this, or he had that advantage. What about the case of two people where all the other things are equal? What's happening there? Lawyer A is very clear. Plumber A is very clear. Doctor A is very clear. It's not about what he's doing. It has nothing to do with what he's doing.

So, be careful that you don't get caught up in a thought that your abundance (or what you might want to call your success in life) will come to you out of what you're doing. It will not. And if you haven't learned that, life will teach you that. Because you'll do all this stuff. You'll be doing this, and doing that, and doing this, and doing that, and doing this, and doing that—and just wind up with a great big pile of do-do. And you'll wonder: "How did I create this pile of do-do here? I did all the right things."

And then it will dawn on you: "Oh, I get it. It has nothing to do with what I'm doing. That isn't the connection. That is not how all this good stuff that I think is going to flow to me, is going to flow to me." And then we see another person down the street who appears to be doing nothing. And abundance is flowing down upon them. Just can't push it away fast enough. That's not fair.

"How does he get to have all that? He's not doing anything." Which is, of course, precisely the secret. He's not doing a damned thing. I mean to say, and I chose my words very carefully there, he's not doing a damned thing. And we've been spending our lives running around doing all these damned things. But he's *being* something. When he walks into the room, he's being something extraordinary. He is being love, compassion, wisdom, humor, sensuality. He's being joy. And he's being One. The highest level of being is: He's being One.

You know, when you go to a doctor, lawyer, plumber, dentist, whoever it is, anybody to whom you're going, the clerk at the post office, doesn't matter—when you're going to that person, you look into their eyes, and you say: "They get me. They see me. They're . . . " in a sense, though you might not articulate it this way, "they're like one with me. This is . . . " We walk away, "What a nice person. What a nice guy. Wasn't she, wasn't she sweet . . . ?"

I always try to get in his line. You know what I'm talking about? You ever have that? When I go to the post office I try to get this one particular guy's line. Because he—I just get a hit off of him. There's just something that—I want to be in that person's line. Because I go through that line, and I just get that hit, that special something that happens.

I finally wrote a letter to the postmaster. I don't know what that guy in the first line has got going for him, but there's a magic going on with him. He makes everybody in that lobby just magnetized and gravitate to where he is.

I asked this guy at the post office whether he feels abundant. I know he feels abundant. And it has nothing to do with his salary. Do you understand? So, that's what makes the difference. That's the difference between lawyer A and lawyer B, plumber A and plumber B. Person A and person B out there on the sidewalk. So, you get to decide whether you choose to be B person, or whether you choose to be A person. If you choose to be A person, person A, and give abundantly of all the magic that lies within you, the magic that lies outside of you will be attracted to you and will become as much a part of you as you allow it to become. Got it? We'll talk more about how that works in just a bit.

So, the important thing for us to remember, when we're searching for right livelihood, is to stop looking for something to do and to start looking for something to be. And to get in touch with that part that resides deep inside of you that knows Who You Really Are. And see what it would take to call that forth in a *beingness* way.

So, look inside. What is it that I'm being, when I feel totally fulfilled and totally self-expressed? What am I being when that happens? Maybe I'm being a healer, maybe I'm being sensual, maybe I'm being creative. Or there's some level or state of beingness that would describe to you in a word or two the essence of what's showing up for you, what part of you that's really showing up big. And that's how we find our right doingness. It's when doingness flows from beingness, rather than us using doingness to *get* to beingness.

I'll explain all of this later, but before I get into it, as I said a minute ago, before I get into a detailed explanation of that, I want to go to some other thoughts, first of all, that I have noticed block people from experiencing abundance. And that have blocked me from experiencing abundance. And I am going to talk about abundance in terms of dollars and cents and physical things. Because it's okay, by the way, to call that abundance, too.

See, I don't want to make it sound as if I'm saying that that's not abundance, and that the only abundance there is, is the stuff we talked about before. It's also okay for us to call this stuff, this physical stuff (the money, and the cash, and the accoutrements, the wonderful glassware and the antiques, and the beautiful physical stuff of life) . . . that's abundance as well. So, we don't want to eliminate that from the category of life experience that we call abundance. And that's another thing that I was doing. I mean, in a sense . . . I called it abundance, all right, but I didn't like it. Let me explain, if I can.

Many people hold the thought that money, per se, is bad. I don't know whether you hold that. And some people hold that thought almost unconsciously. That is to say, if you asked them directly: "Do you experience that money is bad? Is it your thought that money is bad?" they would say, "No, money is good." Many people would say that. But they act as if it's bad.

I'll give you an example. I knew a person who would never admit that she held the idea that money is bad. To her, in fact, money is good. But when she does you a favor, like drive you to the airport, two hours back and forth to Phoenix or something, and you get down to Phoenix, and say, "Let me give you just a couple of dollars for gas," you get: "Oh, no, no, no. I couldn't. I couldn't."

Did you ever have anybody do you a favor, and when you want to offer them a few pennies, just to kind of compensate for some of the hard costs they put into it, they won't take the money? What do you suppose that's about? They're happy to take your thanks. They don't want to take your money. Because somehow the exchange of money for the good thing they did for you, at some level, besmirches the exchange. You see, it drops it to a level that starts to feel icky.

By the way, that level would never feel icky to me. So, if anybody wants to give me money for doing something nice, just let me know. I'll take all the money in the room. That's hard to say sometimes, because people want to think, "Oh, Neale's a really spiritual guy. He shouldn't be saying stuff like that." But I am going to say that stuff.

There's a guy I once knew named Reverend Ike, who used to say, "I *love* money, and money loves *me*." And that's a great message: I love money, and money loves me. And I don't declare that, in my universe, God is everything except money.

Rather, I declare that God is everything, *including money;* that money is just another form of the energy that we call God.

I don't know whether you've been following world news very closely, but they're having this incredible shift of consciousness in Red China, where they're now telling the people about the virtues and the glory of earning and having money, paying your own way, and being self-reliant and self-sufficient. Can you imagine that? This, in Red China—which, by the way, is one of the thirty-seven nations which has translated the *Conversations with God* books. The People's Republic of China, of all places.

You see, the world is changing overnight in every one of its places. So, if the people, the peasants in Red China, are now starting to become clear about the glory and, I want to say, to "coin" a phrase, the okayness of money, and having it, don't you think we should? So, we need to get off of our idea that somehow money is bad.

You know, we talk about filthy lucre, and we talk about being filthy rich. We use phrases that give away what our inner thought is, or at least the inner thought of society at large, about this. And I can tell you that society still holds this thought very deeply. One of the questions I am most frequently asked by people at large, and by lecture audiences, and so forth, and by the media inevitably, when I get interviewed by one of the major media people: "How does it feel for you to be going around the country talking about spirituality, and making so much money at it?" As if somehow I'm doing something wrong, you see. As if somehow that should be a warning to the public . . . big warning. "See, look . . . look at how much money he's making off this."

And every so often I get a letter from somebody who says: "If you're really so spiritual, why don't you give away all of your royalties to the poor? Why don't you, for that matter, just put the book on the Internet, and let people have access to it for free?" And the reason that we don't do that is that if we did that, the publishers would go out of business, and the book could never be produced to begin with.

See, somebody has to do the first thing, called publish the book in some form. And there's a second reason i didn't just put the writing up on the Internet. Who would have read it? It would have gotten lost among the hundreds of thousands of commentaries and opinions and observations posted every day on the Web. Publishing the books through a publishing house legitimizes the work, giving it an entirely different patina than a book-length pile of words just slapped up on the Internet.

So, I refuse to go to that place that says if you were really a spiritual person, you'd give your book away. You'd take the royalties that you do get for it and spread them out among the poor. And you wouldn't take any of that for yourself. As it happens, just as a matter of information, I personally, and the foundation I have created, contribute each year to many worthwhile causes. That's not important. It's just what's true. It's just what's so.

But, you know, I love making a lot of money. Because it allows me to do a lot of things, and I'm very clear what I want to do in the world. I'm very clear the changes that I want to cause to happen. And as I said, in our society, it takes that lubrication to make that occur.

I think we have to forget everything we've ever learned about money. I really think we have to erase the blackboard and wipe the slate completely clean. Even those of us who have been blessed to have a bit of money in our lives sometimes have a hard time dealing with that—and being okay with it. Because virtually every message we've received about money makes money the bad guy, the villain, and by extension, those who have it become the villains in life, even though people are not villains, even those who have a great deal of money. We've got this mind-set about money. Money is the root of all evil. We call it filthy lucre and people who have a lot of it are said to be filthy rich. There's something dirty about it—something unclean. And it's almost as if those who do have a little bit of it maybe got it some way that was undeserving, that it wasn't fair or it's not okay for them to have it. So there's this huge myth about money . . . I call it the money myth. And the money myth in human societies is that it's really not okay, which is interesting, because everyone wants it. So that puts everyone in a position of wanting something that it's very not okay to have.

It's a little bit like sex. It's the same way. I don't know very many people who don't want as much sex, good sex, at least, as they can get. But it's very not okay in most places in our society—see I'm not really joking about this—I'm being quite serious—it's very not okay in our society to want a lot of sex. And if you just come out and say, "I want a lot of sex," people think that somehow you're deranged or you're not okay in some way. Money is the same way—even more so.

You know, if you walk down the street and ask people about their sex lives, they'll actually talk to you about that. But ask them how much they have in their bank account. Watch their face go crazy. "You want to know *what?* What I have in my bank account? I beg your pardon, that's very personal." Who you slept with last night is not [personal]—well a little bit—but this is *really* personal. You're talking about money here. So people have even a more negative charge about money than they do about their own sexuality. Interesting, isn't it? It has to do with all of the messages we've received all of our lives about money—nine-tenths of which have been very, very negative.

So, how to become friends with money? First, you have to forget everything you've ever been told about it. And then you have to put in its place a new message: There's nothing in the universe that isn't God. And God, and the energy which is God, is found in everything, including money. It isn't like God is everywhere except in your billfold. In fact, God *is* everywhere.

We need to understand that money is simply another form of the energy of life, and a very, very powerful form, not powerful in and of itself, but powerful because we've given it power. We, as a society on this planet, have said, "We grant this particular medium of exchange enormous power in our lives." And that should really render it totally okay. We've given it our blessing. We've said that we value this more than that. We value gold, for instance, more than dirt, unless it's dirt in some particular place that can turn into gold very quickly—called real estate. But we have blessed something, and then condemned it, at the same time, you see; it's an interesting contradiction. Again, just as we've done with sex. We bless the act of human love that demonstrates itself in a sexual response at the same time we condemn it. It's extraordinary. All of that behavior springs from an even larger cultural myth. And the larger cultural myth that many religions have given us, I'm sorry to say, is: "You're not to enjoy yourself." And since sex and money are two ways that we can enjoy ourselves, we've made them both wrong—terribly, terribly wrong—and created enormous dysfunction on the planet, and in our own personal lives.

How to make friends with money? Imagine that money was a gift to you from the universe with which to do every good for yourself and for others that you ever wanted to do. Now we have yet another hurdle to get across. "Oh my, if I have a lot of money, I can actually do good things for myself. I could actually go out and buy a very expensive suit, or $550 Italian shoes." Do I dare even say that I'm wearing $550 Italian shoes? Actually I am. Do you know how long it took me to be okay with a pair of $550 Italian shoes? I mean, this is not about the shoe; it's about what this represents in my life. And it doesn't represent that I have the money to afford it. It represents that I have the mind-set to make it okay for me to have this. Do you understand that that's a huge graduation?

I want to share what's made it possible for me to make this graduation. Because this is about more than this sole . . . this is about *this* soul—and the soul in each of us—so that *everyone* can walk, ultimately, in these shoes. Figuratively and literally, everyone can walk in the same shoes . . . when they learn this lesson: There is no part of life whatsoever that is not a part of God. There's no aspect of the life energy whatsoever that is not holy and sacred. Nothing is evil, lest thinking make it so. Let us stop making money evil. Let's stop making sex evil, and most of all, let's stop making each other evil.

What are we doing here? And why are we doing it? Why do we insist on seeing evil and negativity in every corner of our lives? What is that about? That's the question. That's the larger question. That's the central question. And as human beings, we are at a focal point now. We are at a critical juncture—we've come to the cusp with the largest question, which really has nothing to do with money, but with life itself.

Do we see life and all of its elements as essentially evil or as essentially good? That's the question. If we see life as essentially good, we'll solve our problems with money and we'll make money our friend. And then we'll do good things with that money, good things for ourselves because we deserve it. I deserve these shoes. And so do you. And then we'll do good things for others. We'll share the abundance which is ours, and the abundance which is given to us by God, with all those whose lives we touch. And no one will be without anything. There's enough for all of us. And when we choose that, we'll be friends with money, with ourselves, with everyone else, and with God.

So, what we have to do is to get comfortable with money, as we have to also get comfortable, I might add, with our bodies, and with each other. We have to learn to get comfortable with the stuff of life, so that we can say, "Bring all that life is to me, and all that I am a part of, life, I bring to you," and not be ashamed of any part of it. Because God doesn't know from shame.

So, here's your chance to just drop your ideas about money not being okay, about money being somehow bad. This is what causes people to stay in lives of quiet desperation. Because, since they think that money is bad and don't like to take any bad thing for a good deed, they wind up doing a job they hate, that at least they can justify getting money for. So, they spend eight hours a day doing a job they hate, then they do something they love as a volunteer. They go to the hospital, or be the leader of their Boy Scout troop, or whatever they're doing. So, they do what they love for nothing, and they do what they hate because they can accept money for that. Because, after all, who would do that for free? Who would do that for free?

But everything changes when you make a decision to be one of the courageous ones, someone who chooses to make a life, rather than a living. And that's when your whole experience shifts. You create a shift beyond belief when you change your thought about what you're up to here when you decide, in fact, to make a life rather than a living. And that shift is so enormous that everything is altered in your experience, including your experience of money. And make no mistake about it, this is possible. I'm here to tell you that shift happens. Now, we have a question over here . . .

So, a conflict I have with money . . . I also appreciate it, enjoy it, and I used to feel like I would have to do things I didn't want to do to get money. Now I see that's not a problem. But the conflict still left for me is that I feel like, if I have a lot of money, I'm participating in a program or system that leaves the majority of the world on the outs. That would be much more acceptable for me if I knew that everyone in the world had food, everyone in the world had medical care, everyone in the world had housing and clothing. And then money was simply a means to play with more (quote-unquote) unnecessary . . .

I hear every word you're saying. But be careful that you don't use your righteousness about that to deprive yourself of the very empowering instrument that could cause it to happen *through you.* Be very careful that you don't use righteousness to *disempower yourself* from being one of those who can actually *cause that to happen.*

My life is dedicated to creating a world exactly as the one you just described. But I can tell you that I'm far more effective in doing that now than I was when I was denying the very power that would cause me to be able to create those kinds of changes.

One of the biggest traps of the human experience is righteousness. And sometimes we feel we have, I want to call it, a right to be righteous. I mean, we really feel that we have a firm grasp on right and wrong in any particular situation. And within the framework of that relative system of thought, we might, in fact, be dead right about something. It's a very dangerous place to be, though. Because righteousness can block effective action more quickly than just about any other kind of attitude or experience. It stops us from being understanding, you see.

When I think I'm right about something, I can't begin to understand how you could hold a point of view different from me, or how a condition can be allowed to continue. I lose my compassion for the people who created what I'm being righteous about. When I lose my compassion, I lose my ability to make any kind of really effective change for the better. Because no one likes to be made wrong.

It's especially dangerous, I think, for us to become righteous about all the wrong that's being done in the world. Because being terribly righteous about what's wrong in the world is a huge announcement that we don't understand that we've placed it there.

Let me give you an example: How would it serve a great surgeon, or a great doctor, a great physician, to be righteous about all the illness and sickness in the world? How would it serve a wonderful barrister, an extraordinary attorney, to be righteous about all the conflict in the world? I mean, he may want to change the conflict and reduce it, but to be righteous about it, to make it wrong that there is so much conflict, would fly in the face of what he himself is creating in his own reality, in order to experience himself as who he really is.

You see, what we do as human beings is, we set the pins up, then we knock them down. What we do as human beings is, we create the exact, right, and perfect set of circumstances (I'm speaking metaphysically now) to allow us to express a part of ourselves that announces and declares who we really are. If Who I Really Am, for instance, is a healer, I will create, metaphysically, the perfect set of circumstances to allow myself to express "he who heals." I will, therefore, bring into my experience, and even, at some level, *create* in my outer reality, illness.

The opposite of that which I am, that I might express and experience who I am.

The worst thing that could happen to the world's ministers would be for everyone to reform tomorrow. They'd have nothing to say to anyone. So ministers, men and women of the cloth, will spend the rest of their lives, at some deep metaphysical level, creating that which needs to be spiritually healed, in order that they might express and experience who they are. That's why real masters judge not and neither condemn. They go about changing the outer circumstance of their world without condemning it. Because to condemn it is to condemn the very process by which they have been allowed to express a part of themselves that announces and declares the glory of who they are. This is a deep metaphysical mystery, but masters understand it perfectly.

Again, I repeat, that's why masters *never* condemn or judge anything, but simply seek to express a part of themselves that allows the exterior circumstances to shift and to change. On a practical matter, just from a standpoint of practical politics and practical social interaction, righteousness never serves anyone.

One of the most extraordinary public figures of our time, in my personal opinion, is Jimmy Carter. He's a man who moved into very explosive political situations without righteousness. And as a result of that, he changed many of those circumstances for the better, in ways that people who move into those circumstances with righteousness could never do.

And my righteousness or anger as to how the world is, in a lot of ways, is a major obstruction . . .

No question. Every moment of righteousness and every moment of judgment stops you from expressing the grandest idea. Because no one can hear you anyway. When you speak from righteousness or judgment, no one can hear you. But not only do you push away the *power* that would cause you to be able to create, you push away the people that could even *bestow* on you that power. Because no one gets righteousness, *not even those you are trying to help.*

You also said something else interesting. You said that, in the earlier days and times when you contemplated these issues, you would catch yourself doing something you didn't want to do, or thought you had to do things you didn't want to do, in order not to "sell out." Yet no one does anything they don't want to do. Let's get very clear on this. No one does anything they don't want to do—ever. We just do what we want to do, given the results we anticipate it will produce. Then we pretend there was no other way, and convince ourselves to feel bad about the choices we've made. See?

No one does anything they don't want to do. No one. Can anyone in the room think of a time when you did anything at all that you didn't want to do? Can anybody . . . Who would raise their hand now? But, I mean, seriously, is there anyone in the room . . . Raise your hand if you think that there was a time in your life when you did something you did not want to do. Okay, let's go over here . . .

I don't think it's that we don't want to do something. But what I hear around me, and I've learned not to do that from the books, is people saying, "I don't have any other choice."

I think that people think that they don't have any choice, because I know that I've been there for a long time. And I used to say, "I don't have a choice." Because I didn't see, at that point in my life, another choice. But when I read the material, and I understood, as you say, we don't do anything without making a choice, I now make a conscious choice to do and to choose to do, and I even say out loud to myself, "I choose to do that."

Now, first, I choose and then I do. And when I hear, you know, "I don't have a choice," I always want to go in and say, "You know, you made that choice." But I think that in our society, it's really not acceptable. It's like having money. It's like I can't make my choices. It's too good. I don't know if I deserve that . . . I mean, there are more I-don't-have-any-choice people than I-choose-to-do-so [people]. Because it took a lot for me to change that.

There is never a time in life when you do not have a choice, ever. As a matter of fact, you have created the circumstances of your life, including this place that you call no choice, precisely to give you an experience of the choices that you have. You've actually created this apparent roadblock to cause you to notice that there was no roadblock to begin with. And some of you will notice that. And most people will not. And they will allow themselves to live the rest of their lives imagining that they have no choice.

"I had no choice" is the most frequently used rationale for us doing what we wanted to do. We go ahead and do what we want to do in order to either *avoid* a particular outcome or *create* a particular outcome, which is really one and the same thing.

So we do what we want to do, given the circumstances that are in front of us, to either avoid or create an outcome. And then we say, "I had no choice." But you *do* have a choice. And every choice you make, every decision you make, every thought you think, every word you utter, is an announcement and a declaration of who you think you are, and who you choose to be. Every act is an act of self-definition. And you always have a choice. But remember this: no one ever does anything inappropriate, given their model of the world.

So, not only are you always given a choice, you are always making a choice, and you're always making the choice that you think will best produce, or avoid, a given outcome. What you seek is the outcome that will assist you in defining Who You Really Are. That's what you are up to. Now, you may not articulate it in that way, but I assure you, that's what the human soul is up to. And when you begin to see it that way, when you begin to frame it in that way, you see life in a whole different way. And you imagine life to be a grand adventure, because suddenly it becomes an extraordinary adventure—an adventure in self-creation.

Some people feel victimized about money. They don't really understand that they're always at choice in their lives about anything—especially about money. It seems to some people that they are at the whim and whimsy of the winds of fortune, to use perhaps a well-chosen phrase. Or the winds of misfortune, as the case may be. And they see, really, no connection between their monetary situation in life and their consciousness . . . the level of their consciousness. They don't make a connection with what's happening with them financially and how they're creating it . . . yet, I'm telling you that we create everything in our lives.

And so some people say, "You don't understand, Neale, you know I haven't had the opportunities other people have had." They've been disadvantaged, or they don't have the skills, or whatever it is that they imagine stands between themselves and money. I would say to them a number of things: first, money doesn't come to you because of what you do. If you think that money comes to you because of what you do, then, of course, you'll have all of those doingness alibis: "I didn't get my college education," or, "I was disadvantaged to begin with," or, "I haven't had the opportunities you've had"—because you're going to imagine that money flows to you because of something you're doing, rather than something you're being.

Beingness is something that everyone has, regardless of their education, their station in life, their ethnic or cultural background, their social status. Everyone can be loving; everyone can be extraordinary; everyone can be generous and giving and compassionate and friendly. Everyone can be all the things that we pay people big money to be, regardless of what they're doing. See, it doesn't really matter. The lawyers that make the most money, the doctors that make the most money, the ministers that make the most money, the paperboys that make the most money, are the paperboys that show up with an enormous smile on their face, a huge, open heart to everyone whose life they touch. They're the ones that go around and get huge tips from the people they're delivering papers to, and all the other paperboys are wondering how they did that. "Oh, see, you've got a better bike," or, "You have a better family background," or, "You have a better neighborhood," or, "You've got a better route."

No one in life has a better route. All we have to do is share with each other a level of beingness that others recognize as something they want to be touched by, all the time. And if we're willing to do that, it doesn't matter what our doingness in life is. We can be plumbers, paperboys, street cleaners, or corporate presidents. But all the good that comes from life will come to us in life when we are willing to open our heart and share, from a deep level of beingness, the treasure that resides within us, which is called love or, loosely, friendliness. You know, a smile will buy you more goodwill than you could ever imagine.

So I want to say to people who think that they're the victims of their own monetary situations, look at those who have made it in life. And take any cross section of people who have become very, very wealthy—any hundred millionaires—and you'll see an extraordinary cross section. Yes, you'll see some people who had all the advantages, all the cultural and social opportunities, and you'll see many who have not. And look at those who did not have any more than you have now, and ask them how they got from where they were to where you want to be. What is the difference between the two of you? And if they have the articulative skills, they'll tell you the difference: "I was willing to show up, *ta dah!* I was willing to give everything I had inside of me. It didn't matter to me."

Talk to Barbra Streisand sometime. Just chat with her sometime. Ask her about cultural and ethnic background and disadvantages and advantages. Then ask her how she got to this place. Some people call it *chutzpah.* Some people call it magic. Some people call it a certain *joie de vivre.* But what it comes down to, ultimately, is a willingness to just *show up in the space* as the wonderful you that you are, regardless of your story. You do that, and you'll be happy in life. By the way, you'll be happy in life *whether or not you have a lot of money.*

Neale, I wonder if you could tell us why so many spiritual seekers or so-called light workers seem to be up against it financially. Those of

*us who left our corporate jobs and are sort of called to do our right liveli-
hood. And yet the testing ground seems to be: Can you make it through
the financial fire? Why is it that so many of us have that going on?*

Because the moment you declare yourself to be anything,
everything unlike it will come into the space. I'll say that again:
the moment you declare yourself to be anything, everything
unlike it will come into the space. And it has to. It's the law of
the universe.

Why? you ask. Because that's the way the universe works.
And here is why: in the absence of that which you are not, that
which you are, is not.

Did you get that? You're shaking your head, my dear,
and saying, "What is this guy trying to tell me?" I said, "In
the absence of that which you are not, that which you are, is
not." Now, let me give you an example. Are you big and tall
and fat? No. How do you know that you are not big and tall
and fat?

Compared to other people, I seem to be somewhat medium.

So, if big and tall and fat didn't exist, how would you know
that you were not big and tall and fat? Supposing that everyone

looked like you. God, wouldn't that be great? Oh, actually, you all look great just the way you are. Just a little one-liner that I can't resist. But what is your name?

Karen.

Karen. Supposing, just for the sake of this discussion, that everyone looked exactly like you. How would you know how you looked? How would you know how to describe yourself? How would you be able to say: "I'm the one with the long, dark . . . Oh, I see *everyone* has long, dark hair. Okay, I'm the one that's relatively slim, and I'm kind of short. Well, actually, *everyone* is short and kind of . . . " How would you be able to even know who you were? You wouldn't, would you? Not in this relative existence.

Not on the outside.

No, not on the outside. And if everyone were identical on the inside, you wouldn't even know the inside of you. Because you'd all be the same. No? Therefore, I promise you that if you want to have a direct experience of who you are and what you are, you will attract to yourself, like a magnet, everything that you are not. Because in the absence of that which you are not, that which you are is not. Got it? Bingo.

Now the secret, the secret, once you know this, is to not resist it. Because what you resist persists. And what you look at, disappears. What you hold, and embrace, you make your own. What you make your own, no longer resists you.

Neale, there are so many people on this planet who are terrified to leave their corporate jobs for fear that they'll lose their livelihood—all the security they've ever known. What would you say to them?

Some people *are* terrified to leave their corporate jobs. They're trapped in a prison of their own device, because they have this idea that if they leave that corporate setting, or that position that they've worked so hard to attain, then all will be lost. And yet all is lost now, because if it wasn't lost, they wouldn't want to leave. So the key question is not, what will you lose should you remove yourself from that position, but what will you gain? And what even causes you to stop and think about leaving? That's the key question.

When you look at why would they even think about leaving, there must be something not okay with where they are right now. What's missing? It's about filling in the blanks.

And so what I would say to people who are in that place of dilemma, is what I've often said to people: you know, you need to make a life rather than a living. You might be much happier making one-third of your income but coming from a place of beingness that brings joy to your soul.

See, that's the key question for everyone: when do we get to bring joy to our soul? Now, if what you're doing to make a living is bringing joy to your soul, how wonderful for you. But I have to tell you that that is a very small minority of people on this planet. Most people are living lives of quiet desperation, doing what they think they *have* to do in order to survive.

My life has taught me that we don't have to do anything in order to survive. I've always thrown caution to the winds, and I've always done what brought my soul the greatest joy. That has made some of my friends and associates, my family members, and so forth, call me irresponsible from time to time. But to whom do I owe this great sense of responsibility anyway, if not to myself?

So I have refused to be unhappy for very long in any kind of occupation or activity that I was undertaking simply because I thought I had to, in order to maintain a standard of living. And I would do that again today if what I was doing now wasn't making me very happy. Even if I allowed myself to imagine that the happiness of others was my responsibility, how can I begin to make others happy if I'm desperately unhappy in my attempts to do so?

So, what I would say to people who feel trapped is, take a little test. Write down on paper: *Traps I am in.* And then describe the trap that you're in. "I'm in a job that I really don't enjoy, but if I leave it, I won't be able to earn the money that I'm earning, and I won't be able to have all the things that I'm having for myself and the people who depend on me." Okay? That's a trap. Then, "What would happen if I got out of this trap?" And then, after you look at what would happen if you got out of this trap, look at the third level. "What would happen if I did it anyway?" You see? What you'll find out is that the world will keep on spinning without you.

I learned a great lesson from an extraordinary woman many years ago. Her name was Dr. Elisabeth Kübler-Ross, and I came to know her personally. And one day Elisabeth and I were driving down the road together, and I said that I really wanted to do something, but it would require me to quit my job in order to do it, and I didn't think that I could do that for a lot of reasons, not the least of which was there were many other people depending on me to be where I was.

Elisabeth looked at me quite calmly and, in her heavy Swiss accent, said to me, blinking very slowly, "I see, and vhat vould all dees people do, do you sink, if you simply died tomorrow?"

I said, "Well, that's an unfair question, because I'm probably not going to die tomorrow."

And she looked at me, and she said, "No, you're dying right now."

In that moment I decided to live. I decided to live my life. And that was the greatest decision I ever made. And that's what I would say to anyone who feels trapped, whether in a corporate job or in any place in life. How much of your life are you willing to give away? And how much of your life are you willing to reclaim? And once you reclaim your life, how much more do you think you'll have to give to others? Not just of material things, but of the joy and happiness which now resides in your soul.

That's why masters never resist the opposite of who they are, but rather, see it as the grandest blessing. Bring on the opposite, bring on that which I am not. For I will not only welcome that which I am not, I will merge and become so much a part of it, that it will bless that which I am, and cause it to have grand expression. See?

All the universe is a field—a field. Some people call it a morphic field. I call it a field of experience, a field of expression. Life expressing *life itself*. It's a contrasting field, a field of contrasting elements, if you please. And it is only within this field of contrasting elements that any particular element can know and define itself as what it really is. That's true in the relative universe.

Now, in what I have been told is called, in our language, the Realm of the Absolute, such a contrasting field is not necessary—nor is it, for that matter, even possible. Because the Realm of the Absolute is, by definition, absolutely what it is. Do you understand? And there is nothing else. And we call that God. In my language, in my utterances, in my form of expression, we call that God.

In the beginning there was All That Is, and All That Is was all there was. And there was nothing else. There was nothing else except All That Is. And it was very good. But it's All That Was. And there was nothing else.

And yet, It sought to know Itself in Its own experience. And so It looked outside of Itself for something other than what It was, that It might know Itself in Its own experience. But It could find nothing outside of Itself other than what It was. Because there was nothing outside of Itself. And there was nothing other than what It was. Because It was All There Is, and there was nothing else.

How then, to know Itself in Its utter magnificence? And so that which we call God seeks to look outside of Itself, but there was no place outside of Itself to look. It therefore looked within, that It might know Itself—not, incidentally, such a bad idea, should *you* choose to know yourself. Look within, and not without. For those who fail to go within, go without.

And so God looked within, and in the interior of that which is God, did God see all the magnificence for which It searched. And It literally imploded. That is to say, God turned Herself inside-out for us and imploded into a thousand, cozillion, cajillion different parts—going here and there, up and down, left and right. And all of a sudden, here and there, up and down, left and right *were created.* Fast and slow, big and small were suddenly *created* in that glorious moment in that first thought that produced God in Its cajillion elements, each one of the elements racing from the center, at a thing that was now called Speed, and created the illusion that we now call Time. Each of the elements could look back at all the rest of God and say, "Oh, my God, how wondrous Thou art."

And all the other elements of God could likewise look back at the individual element, making that observation, and say to that individual element the exact same thing. Only the individual element has not heard It. The individual element of that which is God has failed to hear the collective of that which is God say to it, "Oh, my God, how wondrous Thou art." And so, that which is the Collective called God leaves it up to the individual elements of God to remind each other: "Do you see how wondrous you are? Oh, my God, how wondrous Thou art."

And when we fail to say that to each other, when we fail to bring each other that message, we fail in the grandest mission of all. For we have come here to know ourselves. We've come here to know ourselves. Yet, I can only know me through you, ultimately, because there's only one of us in the room.

But, should you declare yourself to be abundance personified, that which attracts all the grand abundance of the universe, including money, I assure you that one of the first things that will happen is, you'll have the direct experience of having no money at all. Anybody ever had that experience? The moment you say, "Abundance is mine, sayeth the Lord," as opposed to "vengeance" . . . there's a new bumper sticker huh? "Abundance Is Mine, Sayeth the Lord." Wouldn't that be interesting? The moment you say that, it will appear in your universe as if it's all gone away. And you'll start traveling, by the way, in circles where no one has any money, until you don't anymore, until you meet someone who is fabulously wealthy. And then, everything will change.

What about tithing, contributing 10 percent of income, and what of companies giving 10 percent of their net profits? Could we not shift the economy of this land?

Conversations with God makes a rather extraordinary statement. It says that the day will come on this planet when we will move into a voluntary expression of sharing. And in that voluntary expression, everyone will take 10 percent of their income, voluntarily, and contribute it. Corporations will, individuals will, contribute it to a general fund, which will then be redistributed to people who are in need and to social programs that serve those in need. On the day that we do that, all taxes will disappear from the Earth, because we'll raise more money by simply asking people to voluntarily give 10 percent than we could ever raise with taxes. And no one will ever feel impinged upon, and everyone will give 10 percent of their income, high or low, whether they earn a thousand dollars a week, or a thousand dollars an hour, or a thousand dollars a year. You'll simply give 10 percent to the General Fund. And there will be an income level beneath which we won't ask people to do that; if

Neale Donald Walsch's Little Book of Life

you're only earning a dollar a year, we're not going to ask you to give us the dime.

But the construction, the economic construction, is based on a simple thought: that when you return a portion of what is coming to you to that Whole System, you, of course, enhance and enrich the System itself, and then more can come to you. The obviousness, if I can coin a word . . . that's not really a word, I guess . . . but the obviousness of that is so clear, it's remarkable that we haven't caught on. But there's something even more important that happens when we tithe, whether we tithe to a church, to a synagogue, to our place of worship, or tithe to charities, or in some other way regularly set aside a portion, generally 10 percent, of what we have as income, for someone else.

When we tithe that way as a regular thing, we make an enormous statement to the universe. And that statement is, *there's more where this came from.* There is so much of this that I can literally give away, on a planned basis, 10 percent of it, and not even miss it. And that statement that we make in the universe is a statement of sufficiency, of "enoughness"— and in fact, it produces that in our experience. That's why so many spiritual movements say, tithe, tithe, *tithe,* not because we want to get your money, not even because we need your money, but because *you* need to make that *statement of sufficiency.* And it becomes a cellular command to yourself and to the universe. You really command the universe to produce the response that such actions would necessarily generate. So, tithing becomes a tool with which we instruct the universe about what is true for us.

This leads right into my next question: what lies ahead for the U.S. economy? What can you foresee in the twenty-first century? What might change? And what about the barter system?

You know, I really don't have a personal vision for the twenty-first century. What I know is that tomorrow will be created by the lot of us. My mission is to affect people right here, today, here and now.

If I had to look at the twenty-first century in response to your question, I would say that my grandest vision for the twenty-first century is that first of all, all of us come from two principles—economically, spiritually, politically, socially. We would come from two principles. The first principle is that we are all one. Do you imagine what the invocation of a principle such as that, we are all one, would do to us economically on this planet . . . and politically and spiritually? It would produce such upheaval and such shifting and such change that we almost can't describe it. And it would be all change for the good, for the better, of course. Wars would end, tomorrow. Disagreements would be virtually impossible; certainly disagreements that lead to violence would be very difficult to sustain, given the thought that we are all one.

And I envision that sometime in the next century, and hopefully sooner rather than later, we will construct an economic reality around that basic spiritual truth: there's only one of us. And it is possible to do that. That economic reality would eliminate all thoughts of ownership. *Conversations with God* does go into this a bit, and it talks about a future in which no one will really own anything, but merely be allowed to act as stewards for certain things. You know, in the old days we actually thought we owned not only things, but people. I mean, husbands thought they owned their wives, and husbands and wives thought they owned their children, and it was like that. And so it was very easy to go from there to thinking they owned the plantation or the farm, or whatever.

But in the future we will be just as obvious in our awareness that we do not own the earth any more than we own our children. We've now finally grown to the place where we're clear we don't own each other. Husbands don't own wives;

wives don't own husbands. By the way, that's only dawned on us in the past fifty years—it's not like it's been around for a long time. In the past thirty years, probably, we've gotten clear at last. That's a new thought for most of us cavemen. And we've gone from that thought to finally releasing our sense of ownership over our children and realizing we don't own them any more than we own our spouses.

And now we're getting to a new thought: We don't even own the land beneath us, just because we have a deed to it, much less the sky above us. Some people think like governments and say, "This is our sky . . . how high up is up?"

You know, we had a huge confrontation in the U.N. long ago because satellites were flying over the territorial space of a particular country, leading to extraordinary questions being debated in the U.N.: How high up is up? How much above a certain land area do you own? To the end of the universe, or where? We began to see how ridiculous we were being about it. Then how far down is down, of course? The minerals beneath your ground—are they yours? Does Saudi Arabia, with no offense meant toward any particular place on the earth, actually own the resources beneath the earth, the oil? And if they do, how far down is down? Some would probably argue, to the end of the earth—coming out on the other side.

That means that everybody owns everything, by the way, because if you really own the earth beneath you as far down as you can go, that means you own the earth on the other side of the earth. So, I don't want to make the question ridiculous, or the answer either, but the point is that sooner or later we'll evolve to a level where we understand we don't own anything, and we're simply stewards of it. And when we get to that place, we'll stop despoiling the land, destroying the environment, and doing the kinds of things we're doing to Gaia, to this planet, because we think we have a right to, because, after all, it's ours. "This property is mine. I get to do with it what I want."

I envision an economy in the twenty-first century where the kind of ownership that allows us to destroy something at will, because we bought it, ignoring completely the effects that it has on the rest of us, will no longer be possible.

And then I see a second level to the twenty-first-century economy. I see a place where finally we are clear that there's enough—that there is enough of what we think we need to be happy for us to finally share it.

You know, there's enough right now on the planet; but there are millions of people who would argue with you. They would say: "You know, Neale, you can sit there and talk about sufficiency and enoughness, but we're starving out here. We don't have enough food. We don't have enough shelter. We don't have enough clothing. We don't have enough money. We don't have enough of the good things that you apparently have in abundance in your life."

Well, it's true, they don't have enough, but not because there isn't enough of the stuff around, but rather, because those who have it are not willing to share it. It's no secret that nine-tenths of the world's resources are being held in the hands of one-tenth of the world's people. Is that fair? Is that okay? Is that appropriate in a society which likes to declare itself and describe itself as elevated, as aware, as highly evolved?

By what manner or means, by what level of reasoning, can a society of evolved beings allow themselves to justify one-tenth of the people holding nine-tenths of the resources? Refusing to share them equitably by saying, "You don't understand, it's mine, I bought it, I worked for it, and you can't have it." It's remarkable that the nine-tenths of the world's people who are not allowed easy access to these resources are not revolting more than they are every day and creating more havoc than you could ever even imagine.

It's remarkable, and the only reason they are not in larger numbers is because of the goodness of the human heart, and also, because of the ignorance in which most of the world's people live. That's why there is a great hesitancy on the part of the establishment to allow the world's less fortunate to be educated. You see, knowledge is power, and the more that people know, the more they begin to see how extraordinarily unfair our system of economic distribution, and our distribution of resources, is on this planet.

So I envision an economy in the twenty-first century which looks at the obviousness of all of that and begins to see the unfairness of it as well, and finally, at last, does something about it. And you know what's interesting about all of this, if I can conclude? We *can* do something about it, without necessarily taking away so much from those who currently hold the nine-tenths of the resources that they feel deprived. I can't even begin to tell you how much could be taken from me before I feel deprived.

I lived on the street. I spent nearly a year on the street, picking up cans in the park, living on the five-cent deposit. I've been there. I know the difference between that and where I am right now. And you could take nine-tenths of what I now own and take it away from me, and I still wouldn't be at that level, or even close to it. How much is enough? That's the question that is placed before the one-tenth of the world's people who are holding nine-tenths of the resources. How much is enough? And how much do people have to suffer in order for you to feel that you've got enough? And that, by the way, is not an economic question. *It's a spiritual one.*

To follow up on her question with regard to abundance. In the first book, the notion of manifestation, I guess you would say, proceeds from thought to word to action. And there was a suggestion there that if one wants to begin to manifest, we need to reverse that process. To act as if . . . And I wonder if you'd care to comment on that, as a piggyback to this other conversation.

Yes, while there are three levels—thank you. There are three levels of creation. So, we are each of us three-part beings, made up of body, mind, and spirit—just as God is made up of body, mind, and spirit. So each of us is an individual duplication of the triad of energies that we call God. And that triad, in our language, I call body, mind, and spirit. And so we each have three centers of creation, or three tools of creation: body, mind, and spirit.

What you think, produces energy in the universe, and if you think it often enough and long enough, it will actually produce a physical result in your life. Anyone experience that?

Sure, most of us have. In fact, a guy back in 1946 wrote a huge, best-selling book on this called *The Power of Positive Thinking*. That new-age writer was Dr. Norman Vincent Peale.

Our second level of creation is words. As you speak, say, so will it be done. And so, your word is really a form of energy. You're actually producing energy in the room with what you say. And that energy is creative. If you say something often enough, loudly enough, I promise you it will come to pass. If two or more start saying the same thing, I assure you it will come to pass. And when a whole group of people starts saying the same thing, it cannot help but come to pass. This is called group consciousness, and it's, by the way, why the world is the way it is. Because our collective consciousness has not allowed itself to be raised to the level of the individual consciousness of many of us. So, our job is to raise the collective consciousness.

There is nothing more powerful in the world than collective consciousness. Every teacher from every spiritual tradition on the planet has said, in one form or another, "wherever two or more are gathered." And it is true. The world that we see, and everything that we see in it, was once a thought. And most of the things we see resulted from the thoughts shared by more than one person—by many people. That is entirely true of most of our institutions, our political and educational and spiritual and social constructions, our economic constructions as well. So, if we can shift and change collective consciousness, we can shift and change the paradigm of our entire experience on this planet. That's why everyone is trying to do that. That's what mass media is about. That's what politics is about: shifting and trying to re-create group consciousness.

We now need to see a shift in *how we are trying to shift* the collective consciousness. We've had enough of politics already, and enough social impact on group consciousness. How about some spiritual impact on collective consciousness? If we can create a new collective consciousness of our own spiritual truth, the highest truth that resides within the deepest place inside all of us, we will change the world literally overnight. Overnight!

That's why books like *Conversations with God* are so important to this planet, and such a threat to certain places within the establishment. Because they create a direct pipeline to collective, or group, consciousness.

Is group consciousness important? You bet it is. That's why we have to be very careful what we allow on our television screens and in our movie houses and in the books that we buy. We need to be careful what we're exposing our minds to and what we choose to expose the minds of others to.

The effort should be to create and to re-create, really, a new collective consciousness, and an awareness of the collective. By that I mean a collective awareness of our collective experience. In truth, what I'm saying is, what is needed now is a universal awareness of our oneness—the fact that there really is a single Collective, and that we all belong to it. And nobody is outside of that. And nobody within that collective is better than anyone else. What an extraordinary idea.

Now, our actions, of course, are the third level of creation—that which we do with this huge, huge collection of energy called our body. This is a very gross level of creation—very gross level. I mean, I'm moving the air right now. Just moving your hand through the air is a huge, huge movement of energy here. You can literally push energy toward someone.

Anyone ever come up to you when you weren't feeling well, and just stand there with their hand on your head and do nothing else? And in five minutes, you can begin feeling that—five seconds, sometimes—feeling that warmth, that vibration. And doggone it, sometimes, if you don't say, "I don't know what you just did there, but do I feel good."

Now, of course, if you go even further than that . . . I'll do this here with this lady. If you go even further than that and actually touch each other, incredibly magical things can happen. It's the energy . . . . Incredibly magical things can happen. Because the energy is very gross and not very big. Very heavy, very, very real.

Now, the problem we have in life is that, most often, people think one thing, say a second thing, and do a third. They do not, as the kids would put it, "have it all together." So they think one thing and they do another. Or, they say one thing, and they think another. Or they don't say what they're thinking, or they don't do what they're saying. Now, I know that none of you in this room has ever had that happen to you in your life. But, in my experience, there have been times when I have encountered that conflict between the three centers of my creation. So, I often do not want to tell people what I'm actually thinking, because I'm not real proud of what I'm thinking. Then why are you thinking it? God only knows.

Or, sometimes, lately, I've started to monitor my thoughts. And when I get a thought in there that I no longer choose, that's not really who I am, I don't give it a second thought. I literally don't give it a second thought. I just throw it out. And if you don't give it a second thought, it no longer has power. It's the nice part about this energy, that it's very thin, very ethereal. And you have to keep thinking it, and thinking it, and thinking it, and thinking it over and over again, until it's thought so much that it becomes very heavy with collective energy. That's why Pogo said (Walt Kelly wrote that wonderful comic strip, Pogo), "We have met the enemy and he is us."

So, life begins to change for you when you begin to say what you're thinking and do what you're saying. And then you have it all together. And you start to create from all three centers of creation. And suddenly, you begin to manifest and produce extraordinary results in your life in a very short period of time.

What was the question?

In regards to the message I got from reading that section, in terms of moving from thought, word, action. And the suggestion was that if we reverse that, then that can affect the manifestation that we wanted. And I wanted to have you elaborate and go into more detail about that . . . .

Thank you. Thank you for getting me back on track. Got to be careful with me, because I'll just talk right out of the topic. Actually, I've stayed on the subject, almost. So thought, the most ethereal form, or I want to say, the thinnest—to use a simple word—the thinnest form of this creative energy. And then your word is the next thickest—to use a simple word—the next most dense. And then, of course, your action, I started to say, is a real dense form of moving energy around. So, one of the fastest ways to create something in your physical reality is to reverse the normal process by which we create things.

Usually we create things first by thinking about them. "I think I'll go to that party." And then we say something about it. As in: "Matilda, I'm coming to your party tonight." And then we do something about it, as in showing up at the party. "Here I am. Just as I said I would be." Because I thought the thought this morning. That's generally how we produce things in our reality.

In fact, everything in this room was once a thought in someone's mind. There is nothing that was not once a thought in someone's mind. But, if you really want to play tricks with the universe and create magic with the stuff of life itself, reverse the thought, word, deed, or paradigm. Turn it upside down, and start with the deed. That is to say: act as if.

Now, we've been talking about abundance here during this time we've been sharing. If you want to experience abundance, *be* abundant, and do as abundance does. Therefore, if you have only five dollars left to your name, go to a store and get them transferred, made into singles. Take five singles, and walk down the street, and give a single to each of five people who have even less than you do. And by the way, you will find those people very easily. You will always find, in your experience, someone who has less than you, no matter how little you think you have. Not because the world is such a terrible place, but because *you will create it in your reality* in order to give yourself the experience that I'm talking about.

So, you'll walk down the street. And you'll see . . . now, by the way, when you see this person who has less, don't feel sorry for them. "Get" that you put them there. You created that experience. You put that person in your reality. And this is kind of like you've got to believe in fairy tales, like *Touched by an Angel*. You've got to notice that this is how it happens. Otherwise you'll see that little soul, and you'll start to have pity on that soul. Do not come from pity with anyone. Come from caring, come from love. But get clear: love is not pity. As a matter of fact, pity is about as far from love as you can get. So do not come from pity, but come from compassion.

Compassion says, in your mind, "Oh, there's a person who thinks they don't have what they could have in life. There's a person who still is caught in a belief system that creates a construction around their reality that's other than my own, and other than the Ultimate Truth." And have that compassion, but never have pity.

But also be clear that that person may just have shown up there by prior arrangement. I think I'll play a wino on the street today. In fact, I'll rehearse my role for thirty-six years, so that at four forty-five this afternoon, as Neale Donald Walsch is walking down the street, he can meet me here by prear-rangement, and I can show up this way in his life, to give him an opportunity to notice that he is abundant. And he is going give me that dollar, one of the last five he has, and it's going to shift my reality of life so much. Because, to me, a dollar is an enormous amount of money. I'm getting nickels and dimes from folks on the street out here. This guy's giving me a dollar. And then I'll walk on my way, having fulfilled my contract for thirty-six years to show up that way on that street corner.

Get very clear, nothing happens by accident. We cross each other's paths in the most mysterious ways and find each other again, twenty years later sometimes. And there are more things in Heaven and Earth . . . undreamed of in your philosophy. So, be clear. There are no accidents, and there are no coincidences.

And so you walk down the street, and you give the last of your five dollars away. Now, what happens there? What's going on? You've reversed the thought, word, deed paradigm. You're now doing what the person who comes from abundance would do, and you begin giving away what, an hour before you made that decision, you couldn't imagine giving away, because you thought you didn't have enough. But now you are clear that you have more than enough—so much more, that you choose to give it to others.

Now, as you're giving this away, you're creating in your body, which is a very gross level of energy, an experience. The body is noticing cellularly: "Oh, my gosh, I'm giving this money away. Look at this. I'm even letting it go." It's kind of like in church on Sunday mornings. You know what your thought about your money is. When the basket comes around in church on Sunday morning, and you start pulling out those dollar bills. "I'm giving a whole dollar. Did you see this, Mildred? The basket there. Wow, a great sermon this morning. I'll make it five. Big sermon."

Pull out a twenty. Bring your checkbook out, and write a *hundred.* Let your church know how important it is to you. If you go to church, or go to synagogue, or go to a place of worship, and it serves you, pull out your checkbook and write a check for $150. Do it just once. Let your church, your synagogue, your place of worship, know. "This is how important this place is to me. I spend this kind of money on all kinds of nonsense, much less *sense.* I spend this money on nonsense." And do that wherever you see something that makes sense to you. Give, give, give, of whatever you have to, that which makes sense to you. And you will discover that it makes sense *for* you. *Dollars and sense.*

For that which you give to another, you give to yourself, because what goes around comes around. Money loses its value the moment you try to hang on to it. Money only has value when you're willing to let it go. Get that, for those of you who are saving your money, you're not *saving anything.* You know that it's even true in the world economy? The longer you save money, the less it's worth. To make up for it, we have to have some artificial construction called interest rates in order to convince you that holding on to money allows you to increase its value. You're lucky if the longer you hold on to money, you manage to maintain its value.

No, no, no. Money has its greatest value when it *leaves your hand.* Because it empowers you to be, do, and have something that you choose to be, do, and have. *Money's only value is when it leaves your hand.* But we will create these artificial, as I said, these artificial economic constructions called interest rates, and so forth, to convince you to horde your money. Save a little if you want to. It's all right. I don't save very much myself. I just kind of keep it moving, keep it moving. You know, just keep it going out there.

But the answer to your question is that, when you change the Be-Do-Have Paradigm, you start *acting as if,* and your body begins to understand, at a cellular level, who you think you really are. When I was a kid, my father used to say, "Who the hell do you think you are, anyway?" I spent the rest of my life trying to answer that question. And my body is trying to understand what I think about that.

As my body starts moving into a field of gross energy, it starts moving things around—begins to give things away, for instance. All of a sudden, my body . . . Well, like your hair—you train your hair, huh? I train my hair. I've combed my hair this way now for years. My hair is trained. Your whole body can be trained, not just your hair. Your whole body can be trained like that. And your body starts getting the message: "I have that which I would choose to receive. I already have it." Now, once you cross that huge barrier . . . everything changes. Because you think you don't have it, and you're trying to get that which you do not have, namely more money. But once you get that, you *have* it; then it just becomes a question of how many zeroes are after the first number. Do you understand? And so, you'll discover that what goes around, does, indeed, come around. Not because you performed some real true magic trick of the universe, but because you finally got the Truth of Who You Are. At some universal cosmic level. The universe never says no to your thought about yourself. It only grows it. Did you hear what I just said? I said the universe never says no to your thought about yourself. It only grows it. The universe is really wonderful. Because God grows on you. See, God is like the manure of the universe. I thought I would say something absolutely outrageous. Completely outrageous. Total juxtaposition, to see whether your minds can hold the most outrageous thought. Because—and I meant that in the kindest way—because God is that which makes things grow, makes things grow. And it will make you grow. Does that help a bit?

So whatever it is you think you'd like to be, do, or have, here's the secret, here's the truth: whatever it is you think you would like to be, do, or have, cause *another* to be, do, or have that. See yourself as the *source,* rather than the *recipient,* of what it is you would choose to experience in life. For you are not, in fact, the recipient, but you have been, and always will be, the source. When you imagine yourself to be the source of that which you wish you could receive, you become very *resourceful.* And then, you do become a magician. You do become a magician. You might even be called a "source-er-er."

You still have a question? I'm going to be as clear with you as I possibly can be. What is your question?

I hear that, and I understand it, and I get that. I wondered if you could address the issue that there is a resistance within oneself, that one encounters in doing, because there's still the belief, the fear, that if I give it away, then I won't have it. So, it's the resistance that is the rub, so to speak. And I'm curious to know how you deal with that.

If you want to know what you truly believe, if you want to really get in touch with the belief systems that are, I almost want to say running your life, look at what you're resisting. And most importantly, look at what you're resisting changing.

There's no mystery there; we resist what we don't want to let go of, and what we don't want to let go of is what we truly believe. So, this isn't a mysterious construction; it's stating the obvious. And yet, sometimes it's the most obvious thing that we ignore and don't really take a look at. So I always tell people when I see them mightily resisting any suggestion, any change, any idea, any concept, look to see if that might be a very deeply held truth within you . . . that which you are resisting changing. And then look to see whether holding on to that truth as you are, with such white knuckles, is really serving you. Really take a close look at whether that truth serves you. It's amazing how few of our deeply held truths actually serve us. It's remarkable.

And when I took a kind of survey of the truths that I was holding deeply inside of me and measured them against the question, is it serving me to hold on to this truth? I surprised myself with the number of deeply held truths that I chose to then let go of, right then and there. I've had some remarkable truths in my life, including simplistic ones that are almost embarrassing to announce, like, "I'm not really a very attractive person." I mean physically very attractive.

Let me tell you something about that. I want to share something with you. This has nothing to do with money. But I want to just share this with you. I can recall once, I was with a very, very attractive woman. Beautiful woman. And I was standing in front of a mirror—we were getting ready to go out for the evening; we were sharing home space together. And I looked at her in the mirror and I said, "You know, you're so gorgeous, why would you want to be with a person who looks like me?"

Isn't that an interesting thing to say? Shows you what a low level of self-esteem I had. But I said it anyway, and she shocked me with her response. She was brushing her hair. She threw the brush down on the vanity, took off the earrings that she was just putting on, and threw them down on the countertop, began to take off her necklace—and I said, "What are you doing?"

She said, "I'm not going out with a person who thinks so little . . . " and I thought she was going to say, "of himself." She said, "Who thinks so little of me."

I said, "What? Who thinks so little of you?"

She said, "Do you think I have such horrible taste; is that your thought about me? I want you to know that I have very good taste, and you're insulting me when you ask a question like that."

I never thought about it that way. It's interesting, isn't it? I'm not even sure why I told that story, except that it made it very clear to me that I didn't understand. I had a strange idea about myself that she didn't hold at all.

So, I made this list of these beliefs that I had been resisting changing, everything from the simplistic belief about my not being an attractive person, to *much more* important beliefs: God is not on my side; the world's a tough place to be; everyone is against me; you can't beat the system; to the winner go the spoils; survival of the fittest—very deeply ingrained truths that had been running my life. And it's remarkable, the number of those truths that do not serve me.

So I say to people when I see them resisting something: take a look at that. That's where your truth lies. Then look to see if that truth serves you. I'm willing to wager, eight times out of ten, that that truth no longer serves you. Did it serve you at one time? Possibly. Does it serve you now? I don't think so. Yet what you resist, persists. And only what you look at, and own, can disappear. You make it disappear by simply changing your mind about it.

I just feel the resistance and ignore it. Simply because now I know better. Because what I know is: what you resist persists, and what you look at, disappears. So, whenever I feel resistance to anything, I know that that is where truth lies, just beyond that resistance. Whatever resistance appears anywhere in my reality, I know that just beyond that is where the grandest truth resides. And because I know, I welcome that feeling, you know, that feeling of discomfort. See, life begins at the end of your comfort zone.

Now when I say that life begins at the end of your comfort zone, what I mean is that it is on the other side of your comfort that your challenge will be found . . . your greatest opportunity will be found. The tendency of all of us is to stay comfortable. Not just physically comfortable, but in fact, more often, mentally comfortable. When we're mentally comfortable, we're mentally stagnant as well. We're just, kind of like, blobbing out there, mentally, and spiritually as well. And the excitement in life is at the edge of all of that. It's on the other side of where we are comfortable. The danger of being comfortable, of course, is that we don't grow. We learn nothing, and we do not expand at all. We're comfortable all right, but we have really produced nothing in terms of expansion or growth in the largest part of our life.

So, I always look to see what is making me uncomfortable, and I move into that. Because it is what is making me uncomfortable that will ultimately make me larger and cause me to grow and become a bigger version of myself, a bigger version of Who I Am. Therefore, in my life, anything that makes me uncomfortable, I take a closer look at.

I'll give you one more example: I was watching a movie about eight or ten years ago—it was a foreign film, not American—and there was a very vivid love scene on the screen. It was a very dynamic love scene. There was lots of nudity and lots of specificity in this love scene. And I was getting very uncomfortable about that. I was watching this thing and I thought, "Now, what about this is making me uncomfortable? How come I can watch Sylvester Stallone blow the heads off of people right in front of my face and I don't have any discomfort at all about it? Incredible violence, that I just watch and I'm a bit bemused by it, but I'm not terribly uncomfortable. And yet, here I am watching this scene of sexual love, this scene of passion fulfilled, and there's a part of me that's a bit uncomfortable."

That was about eight or ten years ago, and I looked at that for a long time. What about that was making me uncomfortable? I moved into the question and found some answers that completely changed my whole life and my whole experience of myself around sexuality, around other people, around my willingness to celebrate an aspect of myself that's so much a part of my basic nature.

I also changed my mind about violence. Now I watch violence on the screen and I have the precise, same reaction that I used to have when I watched overt celebrations of sexuality on the screen. Now I can watch those kinds of experiences on the screen with absolute comfort, but when I see just overt violence on the screen, I find myself reeling back and not really enjoying that so much—not even accepting it. I usually actually walk out of the theatre, or turn off the TV.

I just used a simple example there, but the point I'm trying to make is that in my life I've learned to look at whatever makes me uncomfortable, then to move into more of the experience of that, because there's probably something there that I want to heal, or at the very least, closely explore, to see whether it's serving me to be discomforted by that.

So when I say that life begins at the end of your comfort zone, I really mean that. On this side of our comfort zone is not real life, but kind of a slow death. I think people should be uncomfortable at least six times a day. And if you're not, *do something* that makes you uncomfortable. Give a speech, sing a song, dance a dance. Go to see a movie with lots of sexuality in it.

So, in the moment that I start feeling uncomfortable, I say: "Oh, there's that feeling of discomfort again. Yes, yes, bring it on." I'm actually comfortable with my discomfort—if that can make any sense.

Do you understand the Divine Dichotomy? I find comfort in my discomfort, that initial moment of—"Oh, I don't have . . ." or "Not for me." The numbers have gotten larger. I was asked to make a contribution awhile ago to a very important cause, and I wrote a thought down: "Well, you know—practice what you preach." So, I wrote a check for ten thousand dollars to this particular cause. Okay. And I'm writing the check, and I'm going, "Even for me, this is not a small number . . . ." I started breathing heavy, you know. Started breathing heavy. Wrote the check out, actually put it in the envelope. [I'm thinking,] "Should I really mail this?" But that feeling of discomfort, that "Uh, uh, I'm not really sure, I'm not really sure," means I'm absolutely sure. It means that the highest part of myself is speaking to me—in a way that vibrates throughout every cell in my body, that I used to call discomfort, and that I now call a signal from the Divine. Move into that, not away from it.

Every time I have denied myself the experience of my own greatness, it's because I've moved away from, rather than into, my discomfort—and locked myself out from my place of joy. Not once in a while, not now and then. *Every single time.*

Now, there are those among you that say, "But what of caution?" To which I say, "Throw caution to the wind. What can you lose but everything?" And until you're willing to lose it all, you cannot have it all. Because you think it's about holding on to what it is you now have. And that to which you hold on, will slip through your fingers. Yet that which you let go will come back to you sevenfold. Because your holding on to something dearly, for dear life, is the grandest announcement that you think that you are separate from it and everyone else.

See, I'm over here, and you're over there. And I've got this stuff, and I've got to hold on to it.

But your letting *go* is the grandest announcement that you're clear that there's no place where you end and I begin. Therefore, in a very real sense, when I let go of it to you, I give it back to myself.

Here are three words to always remember. Have these words tattooed on your left wrist: *Be the source.*

Neale Donald Walsch's Little Book of Life

Be the source of that which you would choose for another. Come from that place of: I am the source.

If you want more magic in your life, bring more magic into the room with you. If you want more love in your life, bring more love into the room with you. If you want more joy in your life, bring more joy into the room with you.

Be the source, in the lives of others, of that which you would have in your own life.

If you want more money in your life, bring more money into the life of another. Whatever it is you want more of . . . If you want more compassion in your life . . . if you want more wisdom in your life, be the source of wisdom in the life of another. If you want more patience, more understanding, more kindness, more sex . . . the point is, it works. It *works*. It's delicious.

And through this process and the process of beingness, the process of being Who You Really Are, you will bring yourself the experience of right livelihood virtually overnight. And the world will shower upon you all the rewards for which you reached in vain for so many years.

So, allow your doingness to spring from your place of beingness. Be happy, be abundant, be wise, be creative, be understanding, be a leader, be Who You Really Are in every moment of your life. Come from that place, and let your doingness spring from that place. And you'll not only find right livelihood, you will have created for yourself a life, rather than a living.

Part Three

Walking in the World

Introduction

What is it like to walk the path? What does living a whole—and a holy—life look like? Is there a way to take the messages of all the great spiritual literature and live them daily?

These are the questions all seekers ask. The answers have been given to us many times, in many different ways, from many different sources. Still, we are not living them. Mainly, we are not paying attention to the words of those who would offer us spiritual guidance. The result is that we have lost our way. The *world* has lost *its* way. Yet each day that goes by is a day less that you will be here, in the body, on the Earth, doing what you came here to do.

Are you clear what that is? And, is it what you are up to? Or are you losing time, spending most of it still searching, still wandering, still wondering? If so, you are invited to stop it. The answers are here. They have been given to us. All the great Wisdom Traditions contain them. And now they are more accessible than ever before.

No longer are we dependent upon the passing of these truths through oral histories, or a few lost parchments finally found. Now we have mass media and the world wide web. Now we have instant and global distribution of books and tapes and videos. Now we have YouTube and MySpace and Facebook and the rest of the Internet. If we are seekers today, we truly do not have to go far to find that for which we are searching.

In truth, we never *did* have to go far. The answers have always been right there, right inside of us. We've received guidance before, of course. From many sources, not the least of which include our many sacred scriptures: the Qur'an, the Bhagavad Gita, the Tao Te Ching, the Bible, the Dhammapada, the Talmud, the Book of Mormon, the Upanishads, the Pāli Canon, and a hundred other books and writings. The question is not *when* we will be given the answers, but *when will we hear them clearly?*

It *is* possible to live life holistically, and the extraordinary insights in the *Conversations with God* books show us how.

Again. In words just right for this Time and Place in the evolution of our species. So let us return now to my interaction
with that live studio audience in San Francisco. Here is a sum-
mary of what went on there, and of the information that was
exchanged, on the subject of how we might all more effectively
negotiate life in the world of the twenty-first century.

Welcome to the room. Good to have you all here. We're going to talk today, together, about holistic living, what it's like to live as a whole person, and what stops us from living as whole people. We're going to take a look at why we see ourselves as separate—not only from each other, but even separate from within ourselves. And I want to begin by talking a bit about the aspect of our experience of life in this body that we call health.

I was at a place when I began my dialogue with God where my health had reached an all-time low. I mean, literally, my body was falling apart. I had arthritis at a level that was very, very painful a great deal of the time. I also had a very bad case of fibromyalgia. I had some heart difficulties that were continuing to plague me. One year in my life, I even had stomach ulcers. I mean, I just had a lot of stuff going on with my body. Today I feel healthier than I felt ten years ago. And I probably look a bit healthier, too, than I did ten years ago— although it wouldn't have been hard. And so I wanted to just share with you what was given to me in my conversation with God about health.

The first thing that I was told was, I think, one of the most astonishing things I've ever been told about myself. "The difficulty, Neale, with you," God said to me, "is that you simply don't want to live."

And I said: "No, no, no. That's not true. Of course I want to live. What a strange and silly thing to say."

And God said: "No, no, you don't want to live; because if you wanted to live, you wouldn't be behaving the way you're behaving. I know that you think that you want to live, but you can't really want to live. And certainly it's clear that you do not want to live forever, and even forevermore. Because if you did, you wouldn't be doing the things that you're doing."

And I said, "Why, whatever do you mean?" And then God pointed out to me the things that I was doing that gave a signal to the universe that I really didn't care a whole lot about what happened to my body. I'm going to use one simple example, which may touch some of you in this room, unless it doesn't.

I used to smoke. And God said to me: "You cannot smoke and say that you really have a will to live. Because smoking kills you prematurely for sure."

In more than enough cases now—that doesn't have to be proven anymore. So, when you say, "I really have a will to live and want to live a long and vital life," and even as you're saying it, you're inhaling tobacco, you are really flying in the face of all the evidence that suggests that a long and fruitful life is not lived, at least not in the best way that we know how to live it, by doing this kind of thing to your body.

I just used a silly, simple example now. Or, for those of you who are eating extraordinary amounts of red meat . . . I want to say, all things in their proper balance. I know people who eat red meat at virtually every meal of their lives. In fact, they can't imagine a meal without it. And it's okay. There's nothing wrong with that. This is not about right and wrong. It's just about what works and what doesn't work within the framework of the human experience.

Some of our decisions about how we live our lives are not quite as clear-cut as that. They are not only about imbibing too much alcohol, or partaking of hallucinogenic drugs, something as obviously detrimental to us as that. Sometimes they have to do with something much more subtle. A kind of mental diet, or mental ingestion of ideas and thoughts that do not serve us, and do not allow us to maintain healthy lives.

For instance, I found out in my conversations with God that anything other than a totally positive attitude in life can create disease. I was made aware that even the smallest negativities, repeated over and over and over again, indulged in over and over again, will ultimately produce an effect inside the human body, which we will call illness or disease. And I was astonished with the number of times in my life when I found myself being less than positive in my thoughts. Little thoughts like, "Well, I can never win," or, "That will never happen for me," or larger negative thoughts.

And so I learned to begin to control the thoughts that I allow to reside in my mind, so that I wouldn't be surrounded by the negative energies that they attract to me. This is particularly true about my thoughts regarding other people.

When I was a younger man, I not only found myself with great dislikes toward certain people, but, to be really honest with you (I'm very transparent), I allowed myself even to *entertain* such thoughts. I mean, at some level, they even made me feel good.

You know, that's hard to admit, but there was a part of me that just reveled in the anger that I felt toward some people, or the dislike that I allowed myself to experience with regard to certain people. And that anger, and that dislike, which fed a certain part of me, I didn't realize until recently was feeding that part of me with very damaging stuff.

People who are angry, you know—even a little bit, but consistently so—find themselves having heart attacks, find themselves having stomach troubles, find themselves having ulcers, find themselves experiencing negative physical conditions.

Or, to put it another way, I know of very, very few people who are eternally cheerful who are always ill. I suppose there is the exception that proves the rule, but I have to tell you that, in the main, you find that the degree of positivity with which one moves through life is almost always directly in concert or in harmony with the degree to which one expresses and exhibits the experience of healthfulness. And conversely, we find that people who are largely unhealthy, who are constantly having bouts with this, that, or the other, who have chronic illnesses and diseases, are often people who, to some degree or another, have allowed themselves to entertain negative thoughts about life, and have surrounded themselves with negative energies.

Chief among these negative energies is the energy that I want to call (again I use the word) anger, and a new word that I'll add to that, resentment. I'm talking about people who are resentful of others for roles that they have played in their lives prior to now. And people who live in the present moment carrying the pain of those former days and times as if they were happening right here, right now.

I mean, you can sometimes look at somebody, and on a scale of one to ten, you can almost measure the amount of pain that they're carrying around with them. Pain that, no doubt to them—not to make it wrong—no doubt is very real. But also pain which is no longer serving them, and has very little to do with here and now, but has to do with there and then. And these are people who will simply not—because they think that they can't (not that they don't want to, but they absolutely have themselves convinced that they can't)—let go of it.

"Neale, you don't understand; you just don't understand. If what happened to me, happened to you, then you'd understand. But you clearly don't understand." And they won't really allow anyone to take that pain from them, even if they could. Because if they let go of that pain, then they'd be letting go of all of their drama and all of the stuff that justifies the way they are and the way they've been for all these many years. Even though in some cases, it's been eight, ten, fifteen, twenty, thirty years since the original injury or damaging experience occurred.

But to hang on to that, and to make that part of their living reality, through all those days and times, does nothing, of course, but allow the person who did that original damage to continue doing the damage for thirty years—and to do it over and over and over again.

As I said, we've all known people like this, and sometimes, you know, your heart goes out to them. And you say: "What can I do? How can I assist you in noticing that that was then, and this is now, and you don't have to hang on to that?"

I can tell you that nothing damages the human mechanism, the human organism, this biological house that we're in, faster or more profoundly than those kinds of unresolved negative thoughts or emotions that we're carrying around with us from some yester-moment that we think has pretty much decided for us who and what we are, and who and what we are going to be.

So, one of the first steps in holistic living is forgiveness. And I mean that in two ways. Life is not for getting, but it is for giving. And until we've learned the Divine healing, until we've used the balm of forgiveness on our wounds, those wounds will fester inside of us long after the outward scars have apparently disappeared. And we will find ourselves, at thirty-six, or forty-two, or fifty-one, or sixty-three, undergoing enormous physiological challenges, and we won't know where they came from.

I read a story in the paper just yesterday on the plane on the way out here of a forty-one-year-old man who died in New York City of a heart attack. And his girlfriend was calling 911, and she couldn't get anyone to answer, because the system was down for an hour. And he left his body for good. But I thought . . . by all reckoning, all those who knew him, a very healthy guy, forty-one years old. Just left. But there was obviously stuff going on inside of him.

One of the teachings of my conversations with God, and one of the most difficult things I've had to deal with in absorbing and accepting this material is the statement: *All illness is self-created.* Now, that's difficult, because people then want to go to another favorite place of ours, which is the place of self-flagellation and guilt, as in, "Why am I doing this to myself?" As a matter of fact, if there's anything I hate more, I don't know what it is—a person who walks up to you with an attitude when you have an illness or a sickness, and says to you, "Why are you doing that to yourself?" I tell them, "Thank you for sharing." And then I mutter something about the horse they rode in on.

But nevertheless, there is a seed of wisdom, though I don't think the confrontation is very useful. But we might ask ourselves indeed, "Why am I creating that?" But, more importantly and much more to the point, "What would it take for me now to step away from this?" So know that all illness is, at some level, self-created. And once we understand that, we'll understand that even what we would call, I guess, the greatest illness of all, which would be labeled in our experience "death," is also self-created.

I was told, actually, that we don't really have to die, but that all of us have elected, for various sundry reasons, to ultimately leave our physical body. Because, frankly, we're through with it, and we no longer need this particular life and this particular form to achieve and to accomplish what we came here to achieve and to accomplish. Masters who know and understand this leave their bodies very gracefully, just like you take off a piece of clothing you no longer find useful, or step away from any experience that no longer serves you. So masters simply step away from their current bodily form, and say: "So be it, that is the end of that. And now on to the next grand adventure, and the next glorious expression of Who I Really Am."

There's a level of detachment—or disattachment, if you will—from that particular physical form. But while we are holding that form, and while it pleases us to do so, how nice to be able to hold that form from a place of health, and vibrancy, and wonderment in the expression of who we really are. And it is possible to do that by simply obeying some very, very simple rules, the physiological health rules we all know about. Yet there are many of us who simply find it impossible to obey those rules. So the first thing that God said to me in the chapter of *Conversations with God* on health was: "For heaven's sake, take better care of yourself. I mean, you're taking better care of your car than you are of your body. And that's not saying much, by the way.

"You take your car in for checkups more than you take your body in for checkups. And you change the oil in your car more than you change some of your habits, and some of the things you're putting into your body. So, for heaven's sake, take better care of your body."

I just want to give you some very simple, if not to say simplistic, formulas.

Number one, exercise. Do something with your body every day that allows it to feel used and exercised, even just a bit. It's amazing what fifteen or twenty minutes a day (which is not a lot) can do for the human body.

Second, watch what it is that you are putting into your body. Look to see whether it serves you to keep on putting in so much junk. Just completely cut out, for the most part— well, almost—the junk that you're putting into your body, the stuff that just doesn't serve it to be in there. I'm not talking about the obvious stuff: the sugars, the sweets, most of the carbs, and those things that clearly aren't doing us a whole lot of good. I've lost a great deal of weight, in fact, in the past several months, as a result of these new ideas I have about what it serves me to ingest. And so now, I'm a little bit trim and slim, at least compared to where I was a year ago.

Now, it isn't that thin is better, or heavy is not so good. That's not the point. If you feel good at your present weight, then terrific, that's fine. But if you don't feel good at your present weight, if you're starting to walk around a little bit sluggishly, and you don't feel like you're operating at your optimum level, then you may want to take some very simple precautions. So take some simple steps to allow yourself to maintain a higher level of health—exercise, and watching your diet, of course, are the obvious ones, and then, as I said, watching that mental diet as well.

But holistically, it only begins there. It just starts at that rather simplistic level. Holistic living, however, ends, and moves into and toward an expression of the Self that is whole and complete. And then one is said to live a holy life. That means that we operate at all three levels of creation, and from the seven energy levels which we have come to call the chakras of the human bodily system. And holistic living suggests that we don't abandon any of those chakra experiences, or deny any of those energies that flow through us.

Let me talk specifically about the energy that we call the human sexual energy, because a lot has been said about how one lives a holistic life and how one lives a spiritual life.

Some people have suggested that a highly spiritual life requires us to be what you and I would call celibate, or non-sexual, or asexual, if you please—that we would deny our sexual energy. And that people who are overtly sexual, who revel and find great joy in the expression of their human sexuality, are okay, not like bad or wrong, but they're just not really very highly evolved. One day they'll get there, and one day get it, but in the meantime, they're doing what they're doing.

There's a whole school of thought that suggests that holy people have little or nothing to do with sex. As a matter of fact, this school of thought runs rampant through some traditions to such a degree that you are required to denounce and refuse to experience your sexuality in order to call yourself a member of that culture or that substrata of the culture.

I asked God about this, because this is something I wanted to know about. I said, "God, is it true that in order for me to live a really holistic life, and to experience and express the

grandest part of who I am, that I must really, really deny the . . . "
(and I want to say I almost put it like this) "the lowest part of
who I am?" And I don't mean even the lowest part in terms
of the lowest chakra. I mean the lowest part in terms of the
mind-set that I held about it.

It seemed that of all the aspects of myself, this thing I
called my sexuality was the lowest aspect. It was an aspect of
my being that I was willing to own, but not terribly openly,
not very overtly, and not very proudly, except in certain circumstances and in certain moments of my life. And so, I had
this shame about it, this level of embarrassment. I have had
that experience profoundly in my life, where I was embarrassed and ashamed, and I had been made to feel, as a child,
that my social expression was something of which I should at
least be circumspect, if not ashamed. In fact, I remember once,
I was in the early stages of puberty, perhaps twelve or thirteen,
maybe just a bit younger, and I was drawing some pictures of
women, copying pictures out of a magazine, and just reveling
in the, you know, the wonderful curves . . . and just the wonderful little stimulation of that. You know how you do when
you're twelve, and you're just kind of being what you want to
call—here's a clue, by the way—a little bit naughty. Whatever
is naughty about that. But I recall doing this.

And my mom came into the room. And she happened to catch me drawing these pictures of naked ladies. I loved my mother, of course. She was a wonderful person. She's no longer in the body. But I remember the moment well, because I was very, very embarrassed. Because her first reaction was one of being utterly aghast that her son was drawing these naked ladies on this tablet.

She said, "What are you doing?" And the general sense of it was that this was probably something with which I ought not be occupying my mind. And of course, it was *all* that was occupying my mind during that period in my life . . . and for a number of years thereafter, actually. Even to this present day—to some degree . . .

And these days, I can enjoy that. These days, I can laugh and find joy in that part of myself that can admit and acknowledge that I find it still delightful to contemplate the human form, and particularly the human form of a gender opposite of my own. In particular cases, that's where my stimulation lies. That doesn't make it right or wrong. It's just what it is for me.

But it took me the largest part of a half century—imagine that—to go to a place where I didn't feel that, by announcing that, I was declaring that was I somehow less evolved, perhaps a bit less spiritual, perhaps a bit less something or other. And that had to do with many, many episodes—like that moment when my mother caught me red-handed, as it were, drawing these pictures at the age of twelve—a whole slew of those kinds of experiences, in which society allowed me to notice that it was definitely a no-no, that really evolved people didn't have those kinds of experiences.

And it had to do with more than just childish inappropriateness, although there was nothing inappropriate at all about what I was doing. But it had to do with more than just that. It had to do with our adult notions (and I'm going to circle back on this) of what it really is to be evolved and holy; that people who are really in a holy place simply don't engage those energies, and have those kinds of experiences. Well, they do. And perhaps that is what *makes* them holy.

So, when I moved into my conversation with God, I asked the question: "What about this lower chakra energy stuff? Do I have to release that whole experience of myself and just let it go in order to evolve?" I'd heard all these stories about how you must raise the energy, raise the energy—up from the root chakra, through the power chakra, through the heart chakra, into the crown chakra. And then you're living in this wonderful place. And you have nothing to do with anything below your neck. That's how it is for real masters. Real masters don't live below their neck. From the neck up, I am such a master.

And I always wondered: "How can that be? Is that the way God really wants it for us? There's got to be something more than that." And then I learned about how, yes, God says for us to live a holistic life, that we live through all of the energy or chakra centers of the body. We engage fully the root chakra, fully the power chakra. We engage fully the heart chakra. We engage fully the highest chakra of all. We engage fully all of our chakras.

But once we get up here, it's not about getting up here, then letting the bottom five go. See, it's not about cutting it off. But rather it's about . . . I didn't mean cutting that off, in particular—not what I was talking about. And I don't know what you're laughing at. She kind of winced when I said that. I think she has the wrong idea of what I'm discussing here. It's not about, it's not about separating yourself from the . . . stay with me. It's not about separating yourself from those five lower chakras. And just residing in those upper, or in this last one. That isn't what's happening. It's about really bringing that energy up, but also maintaining your connection with all the chakras beneath it. And then you live holistically.

Living a holistic life involves more than even this—more than even purifying your thoughts, or getting rid of negativity;

more than some of the simplistic solutions of living health-fully and watching your diet; more than even living from all of your chakra centers, from the whole part of you.

It involves recontextualizing your whole life, and coming to some new understandings about how the whole thing works. I mean, the whole process that we call life itself. And it involves coming to new clarity about the wholeness of Who You Are, Who You Really Are. Most people are finding it very difficult, in these days and time—and have really from the beginning of time—to live their life from the largest idea of the wholeness of who they really are. And the reason they have difficulty with that is because they're caught in fear. Most people's lives, to one degree or another, are run by fear.

Conversations with God tells us that there are only two places from which every thought, word, or deed springs; that everything we think, say, and do has its origin in either love or fear. And for a great many members of the human race, a great deal of the time, it's fear which controls and creates the thought, the word, and the deed. And so one of our first steps toward moving into wholeness and toward living a holistic life is the step away from fear. You know, the acronym for fear is "false evidence appearing real." There's another acronym, which is "feeling excited and ready."

One of my great teachers shared that with me one day, and said this sentence to me, which I've never forgotten: "Neale, call your fears adventure." Isn't that a great thing to say? Call your fears adventure. When I began to do that, I began to step away from my fear. I also began to look at what it was that I ultimately was afraid of. And of course, what I was ultimately afraid of, at the end of the line, was God. See, I thought that God would never forgive me for all the things that I was or all the things that I was not; for the times that I failed to live up to what I thought was God's idea about who I should be; or for all the times when I behaved in a way that was inappropriate, according to what I imagined God's requirements to be.

And, oh, those requirements have been laid upon me by every segment of my society, and by many, many people in my life. And only when I began to create and to experience my own personal relationship with God could I step away from my fear of God's reaction to the way I've lived my life.

Here is the statement that God would have all of us make, even as we review our litany of supposed offenses: "I am guiltless, and I am innocent. I am guiltless and I am innocent."

That doesn't mean that I've never done anything in my life that I wouldn't do over again a different way. It doesn't even mean that I choose to stand away from a place of responsibility for the outcomes that I helped to co-create. It means, however, that I am guiltless, and I am innocent of any crime.

If being human is a crime, then I'm guilty. If being an evolving entity is a crime, then I am guilty. If growing in awareness, in sensitivity, in understanding in the expression of who I am is a crime, then I'm guilty. But if those things are not crimes, and I assure you in the kingdom of God they are not, then I am guiltless and I am innocent. And God is not going to punish me because somehow I didn't get it right. And least of all, *least of all,* will God punish me because I haven't done it the way *someone else* said was right.

Well, I'll just share with you a personal experience from my childhood. Remember I was born and raised a Roman Catholic, and I was taught at an early age, of course, to make the sign of the cross, which is a uniquely Catholic (although not necessarily Roman Catholic) thing to do. The Greek Orthodox make the sign of the cross as well.

Now, here's what I remember being taught. The sign of the cross, with no disrespect meant to anyone please—don't anyone get nervous about this—was done like this: "In the name of the Father, and of the Son, and of the Holy Spirit" [motions]. Now, the Greek Orthodox, if I have this correctly—if there's a Greek Orthodox in the audience, then I'm sure you'll tell me—do it like this [motions].

Did you notice anything different? I touched this shoulder first, and then went to this one, rather than the other way around. I remember in third grade the nun telling me that this way was wrong, and it didn't work—or at least that was the inference that my third-grade mind got from what she said was the wrong way to make the sign of the cross.

Now, there are a lot of wrong ways to do all sorts of things, you know. There are people that say you have to spread out a carpet and bow to the East at least three times a day. There are people that say that you are supposed to only stand before one particular portion of the Wailing Wall. And if you're a woman, you can't stand with the men. There are people who say that you have to do this particular ritual and that particular ritual, or you cannot go to Heaven. And so we've been filled with these ideas and concepts about what is right and wrong, and what God requires and does not require. And it is remarkable the amount of guilt that we carry with us for the things we have done in our lives. Some of which were really the innocent, pure actings-out of childhood. And that's the saddest thing of all, when even a little child is made to feel guilty about something they've done.

I remember when I was around eleven years old or so that I was having a hamburger, and I suddenly realized, "Oh, my God, it's Friday." I was a very devout, young Catholic boy, and so I thought I had committed a sin, because I had been told that eating meat on Fridays was, in fact, a venial sin. And I remember I was very nervous, because I had done this, and forgot myself for a minute.

My mother took a look at me when I came into the house. I had gotten it at the local fast-food joint. And she said: "What's the matter? Are you okay? Did somebody beat you up? What happened?" And I said: "No, but I ate meat, I ate meat. I forgot it was Friday. God is going to be mad at me." That's what I really, really thought, in my eleven-year-old mind. My heart was breaking that I did this thing, because I was very devout—I was even an altar boy, if you can imagine. What are you laughing at?

And so, I said to my mother: "I had meat. I forgot it was Friday." My mother, God bless her, she just held me in her arms, and she said: "Sweetheart, it's okay. I'm sure it's all right. Don't be upset about it."

Now, my mother was wise enough to know that at the age of eleven, I probably wasn't ready to hear that God simply didn't care. Only years later, when I turned twenty-one, could I even begin to grasp that thought. Because at the age of twenty-one, as it happened, a huge headline found its way to the top of the page of our local paper. And it said, "Pope declares eating meat on Friday no longer a sin." And I thought to myself, "Isn't that wonderful! Now, all those people who ate meat on Fridays can get out of . . . " They never went to Hell, of course, because they wouldn't go to Hell for eating meat. It was simply purgatory, because, eating meat on Fridays was kind of a moral misdemeanor, but it wasn't really a huge crime.

I can take my own particular upbringing, and I hope that you'll give me leave because I speak from my own childhood. All of us can tell stories like that about how we were allowed, whatever our religious background, to be, or made to feel guilty about those kinds of things.

Well, I have to tell you that if it was just limited to small stuff like that (what my father would call small potatoes), it would not be a problem. But the truth is, half the human race is carrying huge guilt about enormous stuff that are simply expressions of the wonder of Who We Are, such as, to touch on the earlier subject, the joyful and celebratory expression of our own sexuality, to name an obvious example of some of the things we've been allowing ourselves to feel guilty about. Or, for that matter, having a lot of money—some people feel very guilty about having a great deal of money. They allow themselves to feel so guilty, they start giving it away like crazy in order to assuage their guilt. "Yeah, I have a lot of money, but I give away a quarter-million dollars a year. I can feel a little bit better about this horrible thing that's happened to me."

And you especially shouldn't have a lot of money if you're teaching the word of God, or doing something else that's really wonderful. So we pay our teachers nothing; we pay our nurses next to nothing. The more valuable a thing is to society, the less we pay. What does that tell you about how guilty we are about any of the good stuff in life, much less about the honest—what I want to call human—mistakes that we make, the errors in judgment, and I mean errors only in the sense that we ourselves wouldn't do it twice, wouldn't do it again?

We beat ourselves up, and self-flagellate, and make ourselves so wrong that if we're not careful, we even create our own Hell on Earth as a result of the mistakes that we've made, and in that way, as well, bring ourselves disease, and fail to live a holistic life.

So one of the grandest, most freedom-giving, most releasing statements you can ever hope to make is: "I am guiltless and innocent." And then come from that place of pureness, that place of wonder, that place of wholeness. Because you can put yourself back together again, like Humpty Dumpty, once you accept your guiltlessness.

Remember what I said earlier in our sharing: forgiveness is the key to wholeness. And now I add an addendum: Forgiveness that starts right here. And in fact, unless the forgiveness starts here, it can't go anywhere. Because you cannot give what you do not have.

Holistic living means living with all of it, the whole of it, the up and the down of it, the left and the right of it, the here and the there, the before and the after, the male and the female of it. All of us have that male and female energy running through us—in, as, and through us. It means disowning none of it, yet simply owning it all, then releasing that which no longer serves us, which no longer makes the highest statement of who we imagine ourselves to be, and then hanging on to the rest, even as we give it away, freely and openly, to all those lives we touch.

Some of the people are going to be bringing up small children. What advice do you have for parents these days? What can we tell them? How can we teach them about God?

You know, the danger of sitting in this chair is imagining that I have an answer for all of these questions. I'm the last person to ask for advice for parents. I'm probably on the top ten list of the world's worst parents. Maybe that makes me a good person to ask, I don't know. I can tell you all the mistakes that I've made. I think, however, that there's one mistake I haven't made. I've never failed to love my children without condition. And to ask nothing of them that I didn't think they wanted to give . . . to me or to life. So I guess the advice I would give to parents is, love them as you would like to be loved. Don't come from expectation. Don't come from any requirement, and most of all, allow them to live their lives.

Release them. Let them go. Let them walk into those walls and make those mistakes. Let them hurt themselves now and then. Pick them up and help them if you can when they have a little owie. But don't try to stop them from living their lives. Give them their freedom—even freedom to do something that's clearly not in their best interests, and that you might even call wrong.

You know, the best advice I could give to parents is to treat your children as God treats us: "Your will for you is my will for you. I give you free choice to make the decisions in life that you wish to make, and I will never stop loving you, no matter what." I wish I had done that with my own parents. I wish I had done that with my own children. I wish I had that kind of relationship, I mean. But we try.

I think the other thing I would say to parents is, don't forget you're a parent. I mean, much of my life I'd really forgotten that I was a parent. In that way I emotionally deserted my children. That's profoundly not okay.

Any final words on the subject of love?

I think love is the most misunderstood emotion in the universe. I don't think half the people know what real love is. And I don't think that half the people on this planet have ever experienced it. If people experienced for one moment what real love is, we could never live the way we live with each other. We couldn't do to each other what we're doing. We couldn't ignore what we're ignoring. We couldn't allow it to be the way it is.

The first problem, of course, is that we haven't learned to love ourselves. That's the first problem. We can only give to another what we have to give. And if we have no love over here, we can't give it over there. These are obvious things to say . . . it's embarrassing to say them, they're so obvious.

What is the final word I would say about love? Try it some time. But if you're gonna try it, try it full out. Full out! Try to love someone just once, just one person without any condition or limitation of any kind. With no expectation, with nothing required in return. Just try, just once to love someone like that. But be careful, because if you do it once, and you feel that feeling, you'll be addicted.

Now, I thought I'd ask the room, because this is a huge subject I'm really trying to button down into a small segment, for any questions, because now is your time, now is your chance to ask any questions you might have at all. Here is the first question right here.

What do you say to people regarding their genes? Everything from being overweight to cancer, . . . Some people feel that they're destined to have cancer based on their past family genetic makeup. What do you say to those people who say that there's no control? It just happens.

As you believe, and as you speak, so will it be done unto you. And there is ample evidence in the annals of medical history of people who have absolutely moved against the grain, if you please, and produced outcomes exactly to the contrary of what their genetic makeup ought to have produced, where genetics, in fact, should have been the controlling factor.

I think it would be foolhardy to suggest that there's no such thing as genetic predisposition. Science has demonstrated otherwise convincingly. And so a genetic predisposition toward a particular condition, for instance, is a reality. But it does not have to be a condition from which there is no escape. It doesn't have to be an inevitability.

Because one has a predisposition toward a certain condition does not mean that we have no control over that. If there were absolutely no control that we could have over our predispositions, mentally, physically, psychologically, we would be said to have predestination; we'd be subject to the whims of fate, as it were—physiological fate, if nothing else. And that simply isn't the condition of the human experience.

Many of our predispositions have been chosen—I mean programmed in. There's a school of thought that says that no one comes into a particular body by mistake. And so it might be said that some of the predispositions that are built into the biomechanical system that we call our body are conditions that we have chosen ahead of time, that we really have selected as tools with which to work, as colors, or brushes with which to paint on the canvas of our life. But we can change those colors any time we want. I mean really, in mid-painting. We could say: "No, I've got too much blue. I think I'm going to go with orange." And we can produce a new canvas, or a new look on the original one.

And so, I think it's important for us to understand that there is no aspect of the human life experience that's more powerful than our idea about it, than our decision and our choice about it, and that nothing is large enough to overcome our cocreative partnership with God.

If God and I decide to change something in the biochemical factory called my body, we'll go ahead and do that, predisposition or not. And really, nothing can stop that process. And it is precisely *by* this process that people have cured themselves of cancer, and turned around other physical and emotional conditions by which they might otherwise have been beset, and imagined themselves to have been fated to experience.

The genes of your body are simply indicators, not unlike astrology, astrological signs. I think that the genes in our body provide us signs, much like astrological signs are provided for the largest body that we call the universe. And so each of us, it's been said, is a universe in miniature. And I think our genes are not unlike astrological signs. That is to say, they can be indicators of directions in which we may travel, but they are not signs of the inevitable. And so our genes simply point the way, indicate a path that could be taken and that, in fact, is most likely to be taken, if you please, unless we change our mind about that.

And if we don't like what our genes are telling us about the direction in which we may go physiologically, we must change our mind about it. It is precisely by this process of changing our mind about the directions in which our genes are sending us that people have overcome so called non-overcomeable conditions—cancer among them, and many others. So we can change our mind whenever we want, and produce a new experience. However, and this is what's critical, not very many people actually believe that. And because very few people believe it, very few people have demonstrated it.

Is it possible for us to overcome either our genetic background or any other environmental condition that should be producing certain outcomes or experiences for us? If it is not, if it is not possible, then the grandest promise of God is a lie, and you do not have free will, and you are not in charge of your own destiny. And we've been told an extraordinary untruth. But I don't believe that. The evidence of my eyes, and the evidence of my life, demonstrates the contrary . . . .

Even before you wrote the three books, and in between each of the books, were you in touch with having conversations with God? In what form did they take?

Before the books became books, before the material came through me, I was not consciously aware of having what we now call conversations with God. No. Only after the material came through—which, by the way, did not come through in the form of a book . . . it was really in the form of a very private dialogue that I was having with myself. But only after that experience began did I become aware.

From that time on, I have been keenly aware that my whole life, and yours as well—is a conversation with God. And that all of us not only *may* have conversations with God, but are having them every day.

One of the questions I'm most frequently asked is, "Why you?" The answer is, it isn't me. I'm not the chosen one. In fact, all of us are having conversations with God every day of our lives. We're simply not knowing it, or not calling them that.

And so, would you begin to see your life, lived, as your conversation with God? When you hear your conversation with God, in the form of the lyrics of the next song that is on the radio, or the story line of the next novel you happen to pick up, or the material in the next magazine article that you find in the barbershop, or the chance utterance of a friend on the street, or indeed, in the form of words that are whispered in your right ear, will you hear and experience all of that as your own personal conversation with God? Then you will have the experience that you ask me about, and that you think that I am the only one who could have.

The important thing to know about conversations with God is that there are some easy steps to follow, should you choose to have those kinds of conversations as part of your reality.

The first step is to openly announce and declare to yourself that it's even possible. How many of you really believe that God can and will talk to you directly on this day of your life? Good. Terrific. Almost all of you in this room. That's great. Because that's the first step—to actually say, "Wait a minute, this is possible, this can be, and in fact is, happening right now."

The second step, after acknowledging the possibility of it, is to allow yourself to believe that you are worthy to be one of those who is able to experience that. We are all able, but very few of us can acknowledge our worthiness. Self-worth is a huge, huge issue among many people, for a lot of the reasons I've talked about in the earlier part of our conversation here.

Much of what we've been taught mitigates against our sense of self-worth, and causes us to feel worth less, worth less than we thought we ought to be worth, so we wind up feeling worthless. And if you think that the feeling of worthlessness is uncommon among people, think again. Many people move through their lives feeling worthless. And so step number two in having your own conversation with God is moving into and accepting as a fact that you are worth it, that you are worthy of such a conversation.

And the third step is, once you acknowledge your worthiness, to notice that the conversation is going on, as I said, all the time. And to stop writing it off as something else, as though it's just a coincidence. Just a coincidence? Let's say I've been worried about this problem for the last few weeks, and I walk into the beauty shop. There's a magazine—for three-and-a-half months it's been sitting there. And I pick it up, and there's this sixteen-page article on the very subject I've been concerned about. What's that about?

I can't tell you how many people have written me letters, saying that this *Conversations with God* fell off the shelf into their hands, or came to them by some other serendipitous route. And you couldn't even believe, I can't tell you how many letters we've received from people who have said: "This book came to me at just the right moment of my life." What's that about? Only when you are deeply aware of how that process has taken place can you begin to understand that this is all part of your own conversation.

But the most important part of the conversation, which we are all capable of having, and which you are all having every day, is not so much what you imagine, understand, or hear God to be saying to you, but what *you* are saying to *God*. And again, I want to say that your end of the conversation with God is your life, lived. The thoughts that you think moment to moment, the words that you speak, the things that you do–this is your conversation. And there is none other. So be careful that you do not say one thing and do another, or think one thing and say another. But have your thoughts, your words, and your deeds all in alignment, so that you are thinking what you are saying what you are doing. And then your conversation will be holy indeed. That is to say, it will be whole. And your life will be holistic.

You have a question?

In the process of bringing that kind of alignment that you were just speaking about into our own lives, could you speak more about what you talked about in Book 3, *how our technology and our consciousness are at such odds with each other, and what our course for the future is going to be?*

Yes. We're at a real crossroads right now. We're at a time, and we've come to this crossroads before, where technology is threatening us, and probably is at this point exceeding our understanding of how to use it. At least, that's true of a great many people, almost too many people at this point, unless we turn things around very quickly. You see, we're also at another point that's fascinating in the evolution of the human species. We are at a point of what Barbara Marx Hubbard called *conscious evolution.* Let me explain.

Until these most recent days and times, the process that we call evolution (the evolution of the species) seemed to be a process that we were, by and large, observing. We were watching our evolution take place right before our eyes. We were seeing the thing happen. Sometimes we did so with, you know, with bemusement. Like I can't believe this. Sometimes we did so with gratitude and excitement. But mostly, we thought of ourselves as watching the process take place around us. It was recorded in history books, and we can read about past evolutionary advances in those books, and so forth.

Only recently, relatively recently, not even throughout the entirety of some of our lives here, but only relatively recently, say, in the past twenty, thirty, or forty years, have we become consciously aware not only of the process of evolution, but of the part that we're playing in it.

Only relatively recently have we become aware that we are *creating* the way in which we are evolving. That's a new level of awareness for most members of the species. And so now we are engaged in a new process called conscious evolution. That is to say, we are beginning to *direct the course and the way* in which we are, as a species, and as individuals, evolving.

This represents a huge shift in the way evolution takes place. You see? It couldn't come at a better time. Because it also happens to be coincident with the time in which our technology is threatening to overcome our ability to use it wisely. For we haven't even yet defined what wisely is.

We talk about such moral dilemmas as cloning, just to use one example, or genetic engineering, to use another. And there are hundreds of them—ways in which our society has created technology that we haven't begun to learn how to use yet. And some technology that is extremely dangerous to our health, to our environment (which is the same thing), and to the way in which we choose to live as *Homo sapiens* on the planet.

So, we need now to take a look at this race against time, and to consciously choose how we seek to evolve with regard to the technologies that have heretofore been driving the engine of our experience. To which technologies do we wish to say: "Just a cotton-picking minute. Just a moment. I don't think so." Can we say yes to this, and no to that? Can we make wise choices and decisions? And can we apply the highest thoughts we hold in common about who we really are, as an overlay on the technological advances and applications that our society permits, allows, creates, encourages, and experiences?

This is the most pressing question, really, of our time. It's not a small question. And those of you in this room, and others like you everywhere, are being called now to the front line of that inquiry.

This is not a question that will be answered by someone else, someplace else, but a question that you will answer. You will answer the question by the products you consume, the individual choices that you make at the supermarket, in the clothing store, on the street where you live.

You will answer these questions in your everyday lives: in what you say to others, in how you encourage others, in what you choose, in the choices that you share, and how you share them. And unless you're really deeply aware of what I'm saying to you, and the implications of what I've just said, you may just write this off as just so much talk.

I encourage you to read an extraordinary book called *The Last Hours of Ancient Sunlight,* by Thom Hartmann. While you're at it, do read Barbara Marx Hubbard's book, *Conscious Evolution.* And if I can work in a third and final one, do not fail to read Marianne Williamson's *Healing the Soul of America.*

These books address this topic very specifically, very dynami-
cally . . . with great articulation, and with wondrous insight.

But give yourself permission to at least move to the level of
awareness that the question invites; an awareness that we are at
the precipice now, as we move through the twenty-first century
and beyond. We are in a race against time. Who will win?

Technology or the human spirit? Technology won once
before, and virtually obliterated human life on this planet—
all but eliminated it. And we, of course, have the ability to do
that again. I want to tell you it's probably not going to happen. We all were afraid it was going to happen in the fifties.
I don't get that it's going to be one big explosion, and that
Manhattan will be destroyed, or that Moscow will be disintegrated by some atom bomb or something. That could happen,
but I don't think that's the way it would happen, if it's going to
happen. It will be insidious things, that seem to take a lifetime
to produce results, with which we will not want to live.

So, I think it's very important for us to begin to pay attention to these slow, but sure, eradications of the quality of our
life. You know, let's stop chopping down the rain forests. Can
we agree on that? It's really relatively simple. And let's start
finding a way that we can feed everyone, so we don't have four
hundred children dying on this planet every single hour.

Question?

Neale, from a holistic health standpoint, what do you think we can do to nurture mind, body, and spirit . . . keep it all in balance?

I think that a real challenge in this day and time is to nurture mind, body, and spirit, simultaneously, and to keep ourselves in balance. That's very difficult in a world which is so out of whack that it often seems out of balance to us. And because the world seems out of balance, we tend to go out of balance with it, as kind of a compensating mechanism: we go out of balance the other way.

For instance, if we're deeply engaged in a spiritual process over a long period of time, say, in a spiritual community, we may go out of balance and start getting very much into our bodies, forgetting altogether that we're spiritual beings. And likewise, if we're deeply involved in a very physical kind of life, which is not receiving a lot of spiritual nourishment, sometimes people do intensive retreats or workshops and seminars, and they go so deeply into the spiritual aspect of their beingness, that they really can't pull out of it. And they wind up riding on a workshop high for six or eight months that bears, really, no resemblance to day-to-day reality, and the reality in which they are living. So the real challenge is to achieve a place of balance. I think it was Gerald Jampolsky who said, "Life is a question of balance."

And the way to achieve that balance is to remember that we are three-part beings, and that no part of our three-part being is more important, or more sacred, than any other part. We are, in fact, body, mind, and spirit.

There are some people who like to suggest that it is the spiritual part of us, our spirit, that is the most sacred, and therefore the most important. That would not be accurate. The spiritual part of Who You Are is no more important, and should be nurtured no more, than the physical or the mental part of you.

And yet, of course, the reverse can also be said. We don't pay enough attention to our bodies. I've said this before. We're not exercising our bodies. We're not keeping our bodies in shape. We're not keeping our bodies well toned. We're paying, really, precious little attention to our bodies in largest measure. That's true for most people. And as a result, particularly in the United States, people tend to be largely overweight, and out of condition. And they die much sooner than they should, because of these and other physical conditions to which they have paid scarce attention.

We also don't pay nearly enough attention to the nurturing of our minds. I'm amazed how few books people read in the average year. I've taken to asking that question of people wherever I go. "How many books have you read in the last year?" If they say three or four, it starts to sound like a lot. You know, I read twenty or thirty, and sometimes fifty, almost a book a week when I'm really voracious. This isn't about bragging, but it's about noticing. I thought that was the average. I thought that's how it was for most people. But if a guy reads three or four books a year, he feels very proud of himself.

The largest way that we nurture our minds, for most people, I regret to say, is turning on the television set. Or maybe going out to see a movie, if you call that nurturing the mind. But the last time the average person went to a library and sat there on a Sunday afternoon to see what Balzac had to say about anything—most people have never done that in their entire lives—in their *entire lives*. And their minds are starving for something other than *The Simpsons,* or the sports pages of the *Los Angeles Times.*

Most people do not nurture their spiritual side, either. They don't meditate. Very few people spend time nurturing the spiritual aspect of themselves in other ways. They don't go to church or synagogue or to a place of worship as regularly as they might, and some, not at all. They don't pay attention to the fact that they are one-third, if you please, spirit. I mean, we're all spirit, but we're three-part beings. And they don't pay 33 percent of their time and attention to the spiritual side of themselves. But most of us nurture one area over the other, rather than all three equally.

Any suggestion on how they can change that?

Stop doing that. The way to change all that is to notice that we are three-part beings and begin to be deliberately attentive to every aspect of yourself, even if it makes you uncomfortable to do so. Move past the edge of your comfort zone.

For those of you who feel uncomfortable in a church or synagogue or spiritual setting or doing meditation, do it anyway. By the way, that's how I began meditation. I was never really terribly comfortable with the idea of sitting down for an hour with a candle or some soft music or in the dead of night, just being quiet with myself. But because I wasn't comfortable with the idea and didn't think, frankly, I even had the stamina to sit there quietly for an hour, I tried it. And I tried it, and I tried it, and then one day I had an extraordinary experience in meditation in which I felt a connectedness to All That Is in such an unbelievable way that I would never now go very long without meditating.

So I discovered something there. It's like discovering that asparagus doesn't really taste bad after all; in fact it tastes quite, quite good, you see. So try it. Move past the edge of your comfort zone.

I'm now, by the way, trying to do this with exercise. Exercise and I have not been very good friends over the years. But I now have a little gymnasium, just a small little room in which I have a few machines in my home, and I'm trying to talk myself into going down there two or three times a week and doing a light workout. I'm sure it would do wonders for me. It's that kind of thing, it's really simple. There's no magic here, there's no mystery. Just give yourself permission to pay attention.

What is the internal guidance system?

Each of us has an internal guidance system by which we can know all there is to know about life. All that's really important to know about life. And if we will listen to that internal guidance system, we'll find ourselves led to the right and perfect people, places, and circumstances that are prepared to give us an opportunity to express the grandest part of Who We Are.

For me, that internal guidance system is not difficult to pay attention to. I feel it in my stomach. I often say to people: "Listen to your tummy. The tummy knows." So here's a process, here's a tool that I want to share with people, that can help them know when they're moving in the right direction, or when they're about to make a wrong decision. It's really quite simple.

First of all, get off dead center. If you find yourself in a place called stuck, you're neither doing this nor that, or shrinking from the decision for fear of making a wrong choice, make some choice. Make any choice. Step toward something.

I always advise people to do that, just move into the process called decision making and step toward something. As soon as you definitely decide to do or not do a thing, to choose or not choose a thing, as soon as you move in one particular direction or another, within moments your tummy will tell you whether or not that's the place you should go. It's an internal guidance system. For me it's in my stomach; for others it's located maybe as a thought in their head. But all of us have that internal guidance system.

You can tell when you're up to something that your whole system is rebelling against and saying, "No, don't do that." And that is not fear. It's a feeling of inner wisdom saying: "I don't really think so. I don't really think you want to do this." Or, an inner knowing that says: "Yes, this, this is the right move. Go, go, go." There's a sense of joy, a *joie de vivre*. The soul is saying: "I'm with you on this. Let's go, let's go for it." And that's an inner feeling, but it comes to you only *after* you've made a decision, not before. And people are often waiting to get that feeling, that guidance, before they make a decision.

Now this is a key point; I want to reiterate this, okay? I know many people who pray and meditate and ask God for guidance before they make a decision. I'm going to turn that whole thing upside down. I'm going to reverse that whole idea. People sit there and they say, "Oh God, please help me. Give me guidance now, before I make this decision." And I'm going to say, "No, no, no; make the decision one way or the other, then listen to the guidance that you're receiving from every cell of your body."

See, it's just the reverse. Don't be afraid of the choice. Make the choice, then you'll know whether you've made the right one. And if it feels wrong to you, stop, turn around, and go back. And if it feels right to you, keep on going. Isn't that an interesting idea?

Neale, I have a couple more questions about the body, primarily regarding suffering. Would you equate a breakdown in the physical body to do with something on a soul level that needs to be healed? You know, metaphysically, they say that if you have a cold, you're confused—that kind of thing. And the other question that I had was about people who are physically in pain, and their spiritual journey. Is it possible for people who are suffering physically to really have this awakening experience when they're in pain, when they're suffering?

Well, the Buddhists say all of life is suffering. And within that context, the answer is clearly yes. Suffering is. Suffering is experience. I mean, what *you* might call suffering, I might not. For instance, I'm a chronic pain patient. There are very few moments of the day when I'm not in pain. I've been in pain throughout this entire presentation. And yet, really, relative to moments when I'm really in pain, I'm not in pain. Can you understand what I'm saying? And somebody who tells you this about me might say: "How does he do that? If I had that pain right now in my body, I wouldn't be able to begin to think straight, much less give this presentation."

I'm not trying to pat myself on the back here. I'm just telling you how it is. And that's how it is with all of us. We all have the same experience here. So, first of all, pain is a relative experience.

To some degree, almost all of us are in pain all the time. When the Buddhists said it, they meant it. Life is pain [laugh].

Because as soon as you find yourself . . . just the very nature of our enclosure in this physical form, really, at some level, is limiting to that degree, given that limitation is a truncation of Who You Really Are, and is, at some level, painful. So, I don't want to skirt away from your question, but just to contextualize it a bit.

Now, to more directly address your question, yes, a person who is in pain can have moments of enormous enlightenment and great spiritual awareness. And sometimes it's the pain that drives them to that. Because physical pain tends to shift our ideas of what's important. And we tend to focus on what's really so, and who we really are.

I remember a time I used to work on the staff of a woman named Elisabeth Kübler-Ross. Does anybody know who she is? Well, I had the pleasure of working with Elisabeth on her staff for a blessed period of my life. And I remember once we went to visit—we often went to visit the homes of the terminally ill. It was a great education. You know, if you really want to have an education, go to the homes of ten dying people in a week. And that's not something that the average person will have the opportunity to do in their lifetime. Perhaps a nurse might, or a doctor, but ordinary people might not have that opportunity.

And I remember one night, we visited this woman who was dying, and she was losing all movement and feeling in her body gradually, from the feet up. It was kind of a degenerative thing. And it would get higher. And every time we went to visit her, more of her functions were lost. Until one day she even lost the functioning of her hand. But she lost it in the moment that she was holding her little granddaughter, who was just a few weeks old. She realized that she couldn't quite move her hand anymore, in the way she used to be able to. So, she had to say, you know, "I don't think I should hold the baby anymore, because I don't feel so confident in my ability to hang on to the baby when she squirms."

But here's what she shared with us about that. Elisabeth said, "How did that feel for you to lose that feeling in your hand? How does that feel?" She was asking her to probe her experience. And the woman said, with the most benign look on her face, "You know, the first time I—the moment I realized that my hand didn't work quite as well as it used to was when I was watching this little eight-week-old angel holding up her hand . . . and delighting in how that all worked." And she said, "To me, it was just like transferring that life from hand to hand."

Now, I'm not saying that that's the way it really is, but that she could find that metaphor in that pain is an example, absolutely, of what I'm talking about. That the level of her incapacitation, and the pain that went with it, drove her to the edge of a realization she may never have otherwise articulated as long as she lived. But she saw something spiritually significant in that moment of what we would call loss. So, is it possible that people in great pain have great insight? I think it is, and I think it's, frankly, rather common.

But you had another question in front of that, which I've completely forgotten.

I was asking about, like, the metaphysical equivalence of what's breaking down in your body. Is there something on a soul level that needs to be healed?

I think, given God's statement to me that all illness is self-created, I believe that that's true. But I don't, frankly, think we should be too terribly concerned with it. And I'm not really into the books that say, "Throbbing left knee . . . selfishness." Okay. I'll be less selfish. You know, "Aching right ear . . . lack of understanding." See, there are some books out now that may or may not be accurate. I'm not putting those books down. But I'm not sure that it serves us to get all caught up in that kind of cause-and-effect relationship, because then we can beat ourselves up. "If I only hadn't been so this and this, then my ear wouldn't be hurting quite so much. Let me try to be more understanding in order to heal the ear." You see? Or, "If I can be more of this, and less of what I used to be, then I'll heal my spleen."

I think the cause-and-effect relationship, while it may be there the way that some of those books indicate, I believe, and I've been told, that it is far more subtle than that. It's very, very subtle, and could have taken place thirty or forty years ago. The original thought, the Sponsoring Thought that produced that inoperable spleen when you're forty-five, could have been a long time ago in a far more subtle way than that of which we are currently aware.

What then is our appropriate response? Love it. Accept it. What you resist, persists. Just move into the acceptance of it, and say, "This is what's happening to me now. My spleen isn't operating. I choose to accept and to bless—bless, bless, *bless* the condition, and don't condemn it. And allow the condition to simply be what it is.

And in that way, in many cases, you'll actually eliminate the condition itself. Because what you resist, persists, and what you own, you can choose to uncreate. But even if what you are owning is not uncreatable, because it's been there too long or the effects are too huge, and it's simply not going to go away; what you can uncreate, and this is profoundly true, is the *negative impact or effect* that it might have on your life. And that's what the lady did with the hand, you see. She saw the blessing in what could have been a tragedy.

I watched a master, whom I knew a little bit in the last few years of his life—I watched him die. I watched him in the last few weeks and months of his life. And this guy was dying a death that other people—again, here we go—other people would have found very painful, very inconvenient, very lacking in dignity. You know, with the catheter and the whole thing. And yet this master was teaching all those who were coming in to see him every day. Four, five, six, and eight students a day were coming to see this guy die. And you had to get an appointment to see this guy die. He was laughing about it. "You know, I'm busier now than I was when I was totally healthy."

And he knew, as did—God bless him—Joseph Cardinal Bernadin of Chicago. See, Cardinal Bernadin knew: "There's one more gift I have to give. In a life filled with the giving of the gifts of who I am, here's one more yet that I have to give. Even my death will be an affirmation of life. Even my going will be an affirmation of the great arrival. Even my pain will be an affirmation of life's grandest joy."

This guy was a master, and I learned from him about graceful dying. And he was able to teach me that, because, while he could not set aside the effects on his body of the prior decisions of his life, *he had no need to.* Because the effects on his body had nothing to do with any effect on his mind.

And when you'd say, "Are you in discomfort?" he would often look at you and say, "Oh, just a little." And you'd say, "How brave, how stoic." In truth, he was not lying. He was really in a little discomfort, whereas I might have been in a great deal of discomfort with the same experience. Because he had moved to a place of mastery, and he very rarely allowed the physical experiences of his life to dictate who he was in that moment. That's very powerful stuff. And we've all known people who have died with such grace. And not only with dignity, but with such a gift for others.

I'll tell you a final story about someone who died like that. My mother was a saint. Everybody's mother was a saint, but my mother was the original saint mother of all time. She really was. And I remember the day that she died, the moment that she died, very clearly. As she was moving into her final moments, they called the priest from the local parish. He was a young guy. They rushed in there, and this guy couldn't have been nineteen-and-a-half years old. I'm not sure that he really shaved yet. But there he was, just out of the seminary. And it was very clear to all of us that this was the first time he had ever administered the last rights of the most holy Roman Catholic Church, because he was fidgeting with his scapular, and all of the oils, and the things that they do, and the things of ritual. And not to make fun of them, because ritual is very important in our collective experience. Be clear about that. Ritual has a hugely important place for all of us. But he had never done this particular ritual with a real-live, dying person. And there he was, going to go into my mother's room. And he went into my mother's room in the unit—what do they call it? Intensive care unit—and a few moments later—ten, fifteen minutes later—he came out white as a ghost. I said: "What? What? What happened?"

He said. "Well, I didn't know if I was doing this all right. And I was getting the wrong oil, and I was trying to get it straight. And your mother looked at me, and said: 'Father, relax. There's no way you can make a mistake here.' She said, 'It's your intention. It's what you bring to the moment. It's your thought that counts, not what you're doing.'" And he looked at me, and tears filled his eyes. He said, "Your mother was consoling me as she died."

And so I will share with you that death need not be a tragedy. And I only hope that when I die, it can hold even a little bit of that grace. And just a tiny particle of that kind of wisdom.

You know, I have a question about the agenda of the soul. In reference to the idea that on some other plane, we . . . plan the places and things and people that we're going to be involved with in this life. I'd just like to know . . . can you comment on that in terms of the idea of why there are no accidents? Is it because we've already planned this on some level?

Yes. Well, I've been told that we do have an agenda when we come into the body, and that it's a shared agenda. And, in fact, I want to let all of you know that none of us are here in this room by accident. All of us decided to be here at this time and place, at some very, very high level. Then we might notice, once again, and support each other in being who we really are.

And here we have come. We have a compact, we have an agreement, and we are fulfilling our parts of that agreement, even as we interact in the way we are interacting on this very day.

That's true, by the way, of people who are being kind to each other, and people who are being unkind to each other. True saintliness and true mastery is noticing that there are no victims and there are no villains, and that the person who is persecuting you is merely playing out an agreement made at a whole different level, so that you might express and experience—announce, declare, become, and then fulfill Who You Really Are. That's why all masters have said, "Judge not, and neither condemn."

And so, yes, we are each of us embarked on journeys that we call this life. And it is a journey, a destination. The destination, we have already determined, but not how we're going to get there. Nor is it guaranteed that we will, in fact, arrive at that destination. We simply have an idea of where we would like to go, and what we would like to do. But there is no pre-destination in the sense that we are guaranteed of arriving there, nor is there any guarantee that the way we get there will be accurately followed.

With each incoming opportunity, we have a chance to move forward with our agenda. If we don't move forward with that agenda, we will, in fact, create other continuing opportunities until we do move forward with that agenda. Anybody ever see repeating patterns in your life? So you'll just keep on doing it, and doing it, and doing it until you get it right. You'll keep on bringing in the same person five times.

Did you hear what I said? I married the same person five times in five different bodies—until I finally got what I was supposed to get about that. And then I was able, finally, to not marry that person anymore. And so, too, has it been with other people and events in my life. Confronting the same kinds of events over and over again, until I didn't anymore; until I finally got what that means. So, we'll pattern it out, and we'll bring into our experience exactly the kinds of people, places, and events we need to bring in, in order to produce the outcomes that our agenda calls for. And it may not all be complete in this lifetime. In fact, I would be surprised if it were. But it is of no matter, because you'll have another lifetime, and another, and another still, and even more until the end of time, which has no end at all. And so it will just continue, and go on and on and on, forever, and even forevermore. Isn't that delicious?

In Book 3, *God talks about highly evolved beings. Should we be trying to operate that way?*

There are such things in the universe as highly evolved beings. I refer to them in my own little short-hand as HEBs, Highly Evolved Beings. And these beings have learned how to coexist with nature and the universe around them joyfully and harmoniously. And they've learned how to live lives that are largely pain-free and struggle-free, and here's how they've done it. It's a two-part formula. And it's a two-part formula that we could apply right here on this planet, if we chose to.

These people currently live off the planet, largely. I have not observed a large number of highly evolved beings on this planet (with the possible exception of those who walk the halls of Congress).

That was a joke.

Here's how highly evolved beings operate. They function on a very simple two-part system. Part one: they observe what's so, and say it. That's part one. In other words, to be simple about it, I observe what's so. You're sitting there in a chair. And we're talking together. Or I observe what's so: television is full of violence. And children spend a lot of time watching television, and then children act out that violent behavior. That's just what's so. Or, tobacco can cause cancer. And because it can cause cancer, it probably isn't the healthiest thing in the world to ingest or to smoke. That's just what's so. So I observe what's so and then I say it. That is to say, I tell the truth about it.

On this planet, most people who observe what's so refuse to announce what they're seeing. In fact, they sometimes say the opposite of what they're seeing, for fear of offending someone or revealing something about themselves that they don't want anyone to know. So, on this planet we observe what's so and then we lie about it. That's a behavior that's common among most people, and very common in our institutions of politics and religion and so forth.

If it doesn't work in highly evolved societies for their offspring to act in violent ways, then they do what works and remove violent influences from the children during their formative years. Therefore, in a highly evolved society, it would be unheard of to place [children] in front of little square boxes for four to eight hours a day and expose them to the very kinds of behaviors that we are asking them not to exhibit. You see, it's really quite simple. It's so simple, it's almost laughable.

In our society, we're doing an amazing number of things that don't work. And it isn't because we don't know that they don't work. The insanity of it is that we are clear that they don't work, and we're doing them anyway. That's the insanity of it. We're clear that they don't work, and we're doing them anyway. Example: we know that it doesn't work to put children in front of that box for several hours a day, exhibiting violent behavior, and expect children not to reflect that behavior. We know that doesn't work, and we do it anyway.

We know that it doesn't work to pour huge amounts of money from special interests into our political system and expect our political system to work without bias. We know that doesn't work, and we do it anyway.

We know that it doesn't work to consume huge amounts of red meat every day of our lives and expect our bodies to react in a way that's healthy. We know that that doesn't work, and we do it anyway. We know, in advance, that it doesn't work to ingest smoke and carcinogens in our system, and yet we do it anyway. And I'm only listing four or five examples. I can give you hundreds of examples like that—probably, if I thought about it, thousands.

Now, the intelligent being has to ask, why? Why would we continue to do these things that we know simply don't work? And the answer is I don't think that we have the courage of our convictions. I think that we're more comfortable saying one thing and doing another. I don't think that we're truly committed to expressing the highest version of who we really are. I think that we're very immature beings.

As sentient beings in the universe go, we're really rather primitive. We simply don't have the willpower to make the highest choice. But we're getting there. We're starting to change. We're seeing some shifting with regard to that, as more and more people are questioning these things that I am talking about. And we're now seeing some spiritual and moral leadership at last on the planet, where we are able to stand up and say, in larger numbers, at last: "Hey, this doesn't work. This simply isn't working." So why don't we do an interesting thing: why don't we just stop it?

Would you speak please to the role of women and, beyond that, the feminine, into the new millennium?

Well, uh—that's a huge topic. And I'm not sure exactly what it is you want me to say about that. I will make this comment, from what I understand and know. At one point in our history, on this planet, we were largely dominated in our society's power structures by what I'm going to call feminine energy. During the period of the matriarchy, it was the female of the species who made the decisions, ran the institutions, and had things largely their way. And that went on, not for a short period of time, but for a rather long period of time. And then, after several thousand years of that, there was kind of a shift in the paradigm, and we wound up with what I'm going to call the patriarchy, where men have largely had their way, and run the institutions, and created the places of power and so forth. In each of those paradigms, it was a process of either one or the other.

And now what's happening, as we move into the new millennium, is that we're seeing this third paradigm, the one for which we've all yearned lo these many thousands of years—a new construction and a new paradigm, in which male and female find themselves co-joined, and in which the roles that traditionally separated men from women are no longer (thank goodness) clearly defined or, specifically assigned, by gender.

Power is shared, and will be increasingly shared between men and women in the years just ahead of us. And we'll find more and more women (thank goodness) moving into places of influence, power, and authority, of creativity, and of impact in our society throughout the world.

We're beginning to see it now, and the day will come when we'll have, as I mentioned in an earlier conversation, a female president, a female pope (if you please), and females in all of the heretofore male-only positions within human society. And blessed be the day. And then we will have both men and women, almost at random, holding these kinds of positions. And we'll find ourselves blessed for that, because there will truly be a balance struck.

This is a balance we've been seeking for a very, very long time. And in the overall scheme of things, in the history of the universe (the universal level), this balance has been struck relatively quickly.

You know, several thousand years is relatively quickly in the billion-year history of the universe. So, rather quickly *Homo sapiens* have been here, and been there, and now they're beginning to strike a balance. Although in our particular experience of it, it feels like it's taking a very, very long time, it's really just a blink of an eye, just a whisper in the life of the universe. And so we've now found, or are beginning to find, this place of balance. And we're seeing it in politics. We're seeing it in our corporations. We're seeing it, really, all over. I'm delighted to see, as I get on airplanes all over America, flight attendants that are male. What used to be a totally female thing to do, for reasons that were never really clear to me, we're seeing males now do.

I have a dentist who is a female, and she's a wonderful dentist. And when I was five, and even ten years old, I don't think you found one female dentist out of a thousand. And so we're starting to see this cross-occupational, cross-gender change, and so forth. And one day we might even allow ourselves to have female priests. Wouldn't it be nice to have, even in the orthodox churches, female rabbis and female ministers?

Soon, we'll begin to share those places of power in the most revered of our institutions: in our religions, in our politics, and in other positions of influence. And as I said, blessed be the day. Because we have been living half a life.

God knows, men haven't done a very good job of running this planet for these past several thousand years. We have not been very effective. And we need that kind of balancing, feminine energy of insight, patience, compassion, deep awareness, and extraordinary sensitivity to the human experience. It's part of the female experience, and of the feminine energy, in all of us. And I hope we'll nurture it, and continue to allow it to flourish as a portion of the largest measure of Who We Are.

How did you discover who you were?

For the largest number of the Earth's people, day-to-day survival is no longer the primary focus. It is for some—too many, frankly—but it is not for the largest number anymore. So now what is the primary focus? The key question before the human race now, therefore, is not how will I survive, but who is it that is surviving? I mean, who am I? *Who am I?* The thinking person seeks to know, begs to know. That is not an empty question. It's an important question, because most people have no idea who they are. I mean, I didn't have any idea who I was until very, very recently.

You know, when I was sixteen years old, I thought I was my hair. I really did. I thought I was my hair, and I was so clear that I was my hair that if my hair didn't turn out just right in the morning, I would throw the brush into the sink and refuse to be seen in public because no one would know who I was, you see.

Actually, not much has changed through the years. I sometimes still wake up in the morning thinking, "You know, I'm my hair."

But when I turned eighteen, I realized that I was not my hair. I came to my eighteenth year filled with the wisdom of that time of my life. And I said to myself: "Isn't it crazy that I once actually thought, 'I'm my hair?' Of course I'm not my hair." At eighteen, I knew the truth. I'm my car. I *knew* that I was my car, because I could sense other kids having ideas about me, thoughts about me, based on what car I was driving. Once, my car wasn't working, and my father said to me: "Well here, take my car tonight. You can have the car for the evening."

I said: "Are you crazy? I wouldn't be caught dead in your car." I mean no one would know *who I was*.

My father drove an Oldsmobile.

Today I drive an Oldsmobile.

And the sins of the father *shall* be visited upon the sons.

But when I turned twenty-one, I grew out of all of that. And at twenty-one, great wisdom befell me. And I realized: "Wait a minute, I'm not my hair. I'm not my car. This is crazy, of course." At twenty-one I knew the truth. I'm my women.

And I want you to know that I played the game called I Am My Women for a very long time. It was a delicious game to play. And I *knew* that I was my women. I could feel the thoughts of people around me in the room. I could feel my *own* thoughts, my own ideas about myself change, depending on whom I did have, or whom I did not have, on my arm.

So I lived I Am My Women for a very long time. And then I thought, one day as I woke up, "Wait a minute, I can't be my women, because if I'm my women, I must have multiple personality disorder." You see, because there were so many of them. So, I realized that there must be something larger than this, that I am. Who am I? Who am I? The mind begs to know.

And then I got clear. Oh, I must have been in my late thirties or very early forties. And suddenly it dawned on me, of course, and I know the time it happened, because my father made a point of it. He said, "The kid's finally grown up." Because I decided, and all of my actions from that point on indicated, that I am my job, as many men at that point in their lives, and some women too, conclude. And boy, I played that game full out. I'm my job. I mean, you know how it looked in my life? It looked like. "Hey, hey, hey, it's my job; it's my work; I have to, I have no choice; this is my work."

Then I woke up to that unreality as well. I looked at myself one day and said: "Wait a minute. I can't be my job. I've been fired seven times. So who am I? Who am I? If I'm not my job . . . "

Then, finally, came the answer. "Of course I'm not my women or my work, or I'm not my car. I'm my family. See?" Now my *mother* said, "He's finally grown up." Because I came to my senses. I rearranged my values. And I played the game called I Am My Family. I'm my children and my spouse and my loved ones. That's who I am. And I played that game full out as well.

And what that looked like was, I didn't take a job in another community—I recall it well—because it wasn't going to be good for my family. I even refused to buy a home that I loved that was just a few blocks away, but was in the wrong school district. And so I made huge life choices, you see, major decisions in life, based on the idea, I am my family.

Then, one day I came home from a job that I despised, from the life of quiet desperation that I was leading, opened the door to my house and found that the house was totally empty—not just of people, but of furniture.

Now, you know something's amiss; I recall the moment very well. This is a true story, by the way. I'm not making this up. And I recall the moment as if it were yesterday. I opened the door. The place was empty. And my first thought was, "My God, we've been robbed." But nobody comes into your house in the middle of the day and takes all the furniture out of the place. Besides, not all the furniture was gone. I looked around and I—I saw, there in the corner, an old hi-fi set that I had brought into the marriage, and there was a coffee table that I brought with me as well, from my old bachelor pad days. And a few of my other . . . my other things were lying around, and I realized that only some of the furniture was gone.

Then it dawned on me what had happened. But I still didn't believe it. I raced upstairs to the master bedroom, you know, and I threw open her side of the closet. All of her clothes were gone. Threw open my side of the closet. All of my clothes were still there. That's when I knew the awful truth. The robber was a woman.

See, it's amazing what the mind will do to stop you from looking at what's right in front of your face. I couldn't laugh about it anymore. I went downstairs and sat there on the carpet of the nearly empty living room, and I cried. "My God, what do you want with me? And who am I?"

See, I thought I was all this. I thought I was all this stuff. And now all this stuff was gone. Who am I? The eternal cry of the human soul. Who am I?

And the answer is not outside of us. Obviously, it's not in the people and the places and the things of life. The answer resides within. And that's the whole message of *Conversations with God.*

I wanted to say, first of all, I really enjoyed reading all three books. They're pretty amazing. And my question is about the idea of the soul. It is on a journey of evolution versus the idea that if it's completely absorbed into the absolute, that there's no more evolution that takes place. What you're speaking of seems to be an expansion of the journey that becomes richer, more dynamic. The vistas are wider. And the idea that you're speaking of . . . the existence of the possibility of transcending that and stepping out of existence, or what we call the process of evolution . . . . So I wonder if you'd speak of that.

You can't step out of the process of evolution. That is literally impossible. The moment you step completely out of the process of evolution, you step out completely of God, since God is a process. God is not a being; God is a process.

God is the process of life itself that we call evolution. And since it's not possible to step completely out of God, it's not possible to step completely out of evolution. Therefore, our evolution, that is to say the evolution of the lot of us, which is God, the Divine Collective, never ends. It always was, is now, and always will be, world without end. Amen.

I want to say to all of you, what a joy, and what a delight it has been to share these moments with you. How good it has been to be here in this same time and place with you. And I invite and encourage you now to go from this place and touch the world with the deepest truth that resides and abides within you. And cause everyone to know who they really are. Give them back to themselves, and let us create together the world of our grandest vision.

Blessed be.

Afterword

For the past fifteen years, all I have wanted to do is help people to understand God (and therefore *life*) more fully, because I see so much sadness and suffering in the world and I know that *it wasn't meant to be this way.*

As I have said now over and over, my deep yearning was brought on by my *Conversations with God* experience—a direct interaction with The Divine that changed my life forever. I have been trying to find a way to *pass on* what I was given to remember through that experience, and that is why I have written twenty-seven books since 1995. Yet even this volume of writing cannot bring these insights into people's lives in the impactful way that personal contact and personal conversation can.

And so I have now put together the *Conversations with God Spiritual Mentoring Program.* My intention is to personally walk each participant through a three-month exploration of the principal points in the *Conversations with God* messages, in three separate categories covering thirty days each.

In this program we will explore Mastering Change, Mastering Happiness, and Mastering Now in thirty-six individual lessons, three each week. Once each month I'll get on a personal call with you *and with you alone* to discuss what you have learned—and most importantly, how to apply it in your daily life.

You'll also have three group conversations joining other participants each month and my hand-selected and personally trained *Conversations with God* Life Coaches—dear friends who have worked with me for years and who understand the material as well as I do. And . . . once a month I will facilitate a call with all participants, so that we can talk together about challenges mutually confronted, sharing ideas about new directions and solutions.

It's time now for all of us to end our battles with those old demons of fear, anger, resentment, frustration, disappointment, and debilitating emotional pain. The aim of the *Spiritual Mentoring Program* is to end those negative experiences, to turn life into what it was *always intended to be*: an expression of true Self-Realization from a place of deep inner peace and harmony, thanks to a richer understanding of life's process and purpose.

I hope you will undertake this journey with me. It will require a significant dedication of your time and resources, but the rewards can be great. Perhaps greater than you might ever have imagined. To learn more, visit:

www.nealedonaldwalsch.com/index.php?p=Doc&c=mentor

I would like to also tell you about the Homecoming, a different kind of program that offers me a chance to sit down with people in a way that is extremely informal, with no rigid program or agenda, no end product, and no outcome that anyone is attempting to produce—only the pure and unencumbered experience that maximum synergy and total freedom from form could eventuate. It is, in short, an open-ended discussion, a grand exploration, both a discourse and an exchange, with a handful of people (never more than fourteen, often less) just twice a year in my own home.

This experience is one of sitting down with me each afternoon and evening in the living room of my house in Ashland, Oregon, for free-flowing conversation and exploration. Shared sleeping accommodations (two beds to a room) are in the home, and all meals are also provided. Saturday evening the group dines out together at one of Ashland's wonderful restaurants, then takes in a performance at the world-famous Oregon Shakespeare Festival.

The five days offer unparalleled personal access to the material contained in the nine *Conversations with God* books (and to anything else that anyone wants to touch upon or look at deeply). The Homecoming is a limited opportunity for a limited number of people who feel they have the time, energy, personal resources, ability, and the desire to co-create such a singular experience.

More information may be had by putting "Homecoming" in the subject line and sending an email to me personally at:

neale@nealedonaldwalsch.com

Finally, it strikes me that after reading this text you may yearn to know how, in a practical sense, to experience what I have called your True Self and to *come from* that experience, in the living of your life—and yet not everyone is able to attend a retreat or a special gathering in my home. So I am happy to tell you that now there has emerged from the *Conversations with God* cosmology an actual *technology* that makes it possible for all of us to live spirit-centered, joyful lives. This technology is described in wonderful detail in *When Everything Changes, Change Everything*, a book that rose to the *New York Times* bestseller list two weeks after its publication.

This book offers a remarkable combination of modern psychology and contemporary spirituality in an excursion of life-altering impact. If your own life has been touched in recent years by unexpected, unbidden, unwanted change, forcing you to encounter life in a brand new way, this writing could be extraordinarily helpful. As will be its companion, the *WECCE Workbook and Study Guide*. WECCE is the acronym for *When Everything Changes, Change Everything*, and the *Workbook* is a seventy-five-page supplement that offers exercises, processes, experiments, and assignments explaining the WECCE technology and helping you to place *on the ground in everyday life* all of the most important insights in the larger text.

If you are comfortable with a more interactive process, we now produce several Change Everything Spiritual Renewal Retreats, attended by people from all over the world. Based on the messages in *Conversations with God*, they are designed especially for those who are looking closely at the lives they are currently experiencing and seeking ways that they can bring about a real shift in their experience.

To obtain a copy of *When Everything Changes, Change Everything,* or for more information on these retreats, simply go to:

www.nealedonaldwalsch.com

Many questions on all of the issues covered in the material you have just read here are addressed in the Ask Neale section of the Messenger's Circle at the above website. If you would like to stay connected with the energy of *Conversations with God,* you may do so easily by joining the Messenger's Circle at that site.

Thank you for letting me tell you about these opportunities. By these and other means, I hope that we can all learn even more about holistic living, about right livelihood, about wonderful relationships, and about all the things we have explored here.

Once upon a time, all of us lived in a happy, joyful, wonderfully expressive way. We moved through our days and times feeling whole, living whole, and being whole. We understood ourselves to be part of a Whole System, and we did nothing individually that would negatively affect us collectively. We knew how to live without expectation, without fear, without neediness, and without having to have power over someone, or to be somehow better than another. If we can get back to that place, we can heal our lives, and heal the world.

We can turn Fear into Excitement, Worry into Wonder, Expectation into Anticipation, Resistance into Acceptance, Disappointment into Detachment, Enragement into Engagement, Addiction into Preference, Requirement into Contentment, Judgment into Observation, Sadness into Happiness, Thought into Presence, Reaction into Response, and a Time of Turmoil into a Time of Peace. That is the promise of the book *When Everything Changes, Change Everything,* that is the purpose of the Spiritual Mentoring Program, and that is the potential of the Homecoming.

The time to bring the life-altering, reality-shifting messages of *Conversations with God* into your life in a more profound and impactful way is now. I hope you will accept the invitation to do so with one of the tools offered above.

With love and caring,

Neale Donald Walsch
Ashland, Oregon
July 2010